Summer Fit™
Exercises for the Brain and Body While Away from School

HEY KIDS!
School is out! It's time for fun!

You might be thinking to yourself, "Fun? I thought this book was about reading, writing, and math. Who's talking about fun?"

We are!

Keeping your brain active and your body growing is fun with *Summer Fit* activities and exercises. We promise to help you remember all the great stuff you learned last year, get you outside to enjoy summertime, and prepare you for the year ahead!

It might feel like a million years from now, but pretty soon you will be sitting at a new desk in a new classroom on the first day of a new school year. With *Summer Fit*, take a seat in that desk smarter and healthier!

Have fun this summer and keep on moving!

TESTIMONIALS
Summer Fit Workbook Series

*"**Summer Fit** is an exciting resource because it incorporates what we know from research evidence about combating summer learning loss, supporting youth development, and engaging parents. **Summer Fit** provides a perfect blend of learning experiences that are focused on the physical, social, emotional and cognitive growth and development of all participants and will be a boon for parents, educators, and other community-based organizations serving youth."*

Cori A. Groth, Ph.D.
Board President, Utah Afterschool Network
Senior Policy Associate, Utah Education Policy Center

*"**Summer Fit** is a great way to get kids moving during the summer! USA Cycling wants to see more kids on bikes and having fun while exercising. **Summer Fit** is a refreshing and fun to way encourage kids to get outside and ride while still supporting them academically."*

Sean Petty
Chief Operating Officer
USA Cycling

*"**Summer Fit** is now the most comprehensive summer workbook available. I love the inclusion of a daily fitness program and cannot say enough how much I believe in the core values portion of this book. **Summer Fit** is fun, easy to use and is a great next step in the world of summer learning. I support Summer Fit 100%!"*

Carla Fisher
Original Author of Summer Bridge Activities
Editions: 1993-2009

*"In working for a company that's lucky enough to be hands-on with kids every day, I see firsthand the importance of physical fitness from an early age. With many schools losing their physical education program, as well as, the lack of nutritional information taught to kids, it is great to see something like **Summer Fit** come out that gives parents a tool to utilize that also incorporates the importance of values. **Summer Fit** encourages involvement, motivation and having fun – what a great way to spend your summer!"*

Katie Baltz
National Children's Training Specialist

summerfitlearning.com

*"This was my first year teaching and I was shocked to see how many students in my classroom are not physically active on a daily basis. **Summer Fit** provides parents with an easy to use program that keeps them reading and engaged during the summer, while equally important, active and playing!"*

Kelly Toblon
Elementary Teacher
Walnut Creek, CA

*"I use a values-based approach to coach 10-12 year old girls in track. Regardless of age or sport, children need to learn what it means to have courage and determination but also to be kind and generous. Whether you are coaching or teaching, it is increasingly important to help children develop socially. **Summer Fit** is a great resource that incorporates values with learning and exercise that will positively impact the over all development of a child."*

Catherine Raney-Norman
Speed Skater for USA
US All-Around Champion 1999, 2002, 2003

*"The **Summer Fit** series leaps forward in the summer workbook arena by providing content that invokes value-based conversations between parent and child within its core teaching and review of basic skills. The fitness component addresses our nations health crisis by helping children foster a positive attitude towards fitness and instilling that "fit mind, fit body" go hand in hand. The addition of historic and modern day heroes provide rich culture and inspiration. BRAVO!!! **Summer Fit** will be in front and center in my retail stores this summer!"*

Pamela Koutsaftis
Specialty Educators Marketplace
President
Cleveland, Ohio

*"I have been in the entertainment industry making movies for families and young people for over 35 years and it is a rare to run into an educational workbook that is so relevant to both parents and children and presented in such a fun and engaging way for both. **Summer Fit** speaks to today's families and uses the world of technology and print to bridge the worlds of fitness and education. It is cool, it is fun and above all will make a difference in the lives of children who use it."*

Tim Nelson
Feature Films for Families
Holy Cow! Productions

summerfitlearning.com

Table of Contents

Dear Parents and Guardians,

Summer Fit is a new summer workbook series designed to keep children academically <u>and</u> physically engaged between grade levels, *Summer Fit* uses an active and values-based approach to summer learning.

Research shows that the more children play outside the classroom, the better children perform inside the classroom. Written by some of today's most energetic and engaged educators, *Summer Fit* creates an active learning environment using physical and academic exercises. Grade-appropriate activities focus on reading, writing, language arts and math, while incorporating physical fitness exercises on a daily basis. To reinforce and teach core-values, *Summer Fit* includes values-based activities highlighting some of the world's most inspiring leaders and humanitarians such as Abraham Lincoln, Mother Teresa, Rosa Parks, Terry Fox and Mahatma Gandhi.

Each *Summer Fit* workbook includes a 10-week motivational calendar to help you create a routine, give children choices and reward both academic and physical accomplishments.

Summer Fit Includes:

- Daily activities and exercises for a 10-week program.
- Weekly values-based activities that inspire children and teach core values.
- FREE downloads to provide extra challenge in reading, writing, and math.
- Bicycle maintenance and safety activities by *Mike and The Bike*
- Reading and mathematics activities based on national standards.
- On-line videos to show children how to properly perform fitness exercises.
- Activities and exercises that progress in difficulty so children are not overwhelmed.

Summer Fit's additional resources include online book report templates, educational games, and information from summer learning partners to help make summer fun and active!

Have fun learning and playing this summer with *Summer Fit*!

Sincerely,

Educators, Trainers and Active Parents of Summer Fit

Educators, Trainers and Active Parents of *Summer Fit*

How to Use Summer Fit

The activities and exercises in *Summer Fit* will take 20-30 minutes a day to complete. Each day offers a simple and fun routine that reinforces skills in reading, math, language arts, and physical fitness plus a weekly core value. At the start of each week spend 10 minutes with your child to talk about the upcoming week (this is also a good time to review the previous week). Set the weekly goal and fill in the incentive that your child is working towards on the **Incentive Contract**. You are now a player-coach, this means you "play" and you "coach!" Participate and have fun with your child and give the encouragement they need to complete the week!

SUMMER FIT TIPS			
Create a Routine	**Go Online**	**Motivate**	**Have Fun**
Set a time and a place for your child to complete their one page of *Summer Fit* activities and exercises each day.	Strive to create balance. Use online resources along with workbook based learning to reinforce classroom skills.	Inspire your child to complete their daily activities and exercises. Get excited and support their mental and physical accomplishments!	Slap a high 5, jump up and down, shout out loud about how great a job your child is doing! Show them how fun being active is and they will have fun being active themselves!

Icon Language

Icons are used throughout the book to represent the different types of skills and fitness activities being taught and reviewed. The **Mind** icon represents basic skills in reading, writing, math, and language arts; the **Body** icon represents physical fitness exercises, and the **Values** icon represents the weekly core value.

Mind   **Body**   **Values**   **Aerobic**   **Strength**   **Sport**

Fitness icons include an **Aerobic** icon for aerobic exercises; a **Strength** icon for strength and conditioning exercises, and a **Sport** icon that represents a sport or physical fitness game. A Fitness Index is located in the introduction with activities and exercises for each of the designated icon categories.

Incentive Contract

Discuss the weekly Incentive Contracts with your child. Each time your child completes the daily brain and body activities, and values activity, he/she checks a box next to that icon. When all the boxes are checked, it is time for the reward! Rewards should be fun and can be as simple as going swimming, having a favorite treat, or going to the park.

Bonus Parent Redemption: When your child completes his/her activities you reward their accomplishment by performing one of the physical activities yourself: "Go ahead mom, give me 10 jumping jacks!"

FREE Downloads and On line Educational Games

FREE downloads are available at www.summerfitlearning.com that provide extra challenge from the grade ahead in reading, writing and math. These activities are designed to be a little more difficult and can be used as bonus activities or additional daily practice. Children also have access to FREE online educational games in reading, writing and math. Parents and guardians have an option to purchase additional online games to help reinforce basic skills during the school year.

Physical Fitness Improves the Brain

Exercise stimulates healthy physical <u>and</u> mental growth. Activities such as walking, running and riding a bicycle have long been used to get blood flowing and burn sugars and fat, but research shows that in addition to improving your body, exercise also stimulates the growth of new brain cells and improves overall memory and ability to learn.

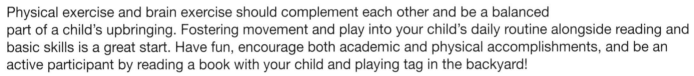

Exercise improves circulation, increases blood flow to the brain, raises endorphin levels, and stimulates the nervous system. This in turn allows children to think more clearly and perform better physically and academically. Research shows that exercise can reduce your child's stress, improve your child's mood, and also improve your child's academic achievement.

Physical exercise and brain exercise should complement each other and be a balanced part of a child's upbringing. Fostering movement and play into your child's daily routine alongside reading and basic skills is a great start. Have fun, encourage both academic and physical accomplishments, and be an active participant by reading a book with your child and playing tag in the backyard!

Exercise is good for growing children, and the earlier they start, the better. It is okay if children are not interested in certain sports. Encourage them to try them all and then focus on the sports and activities they have fun playing. Try to maintain a healthy balance between outside and inside play time and include video games that are designed to get kids moving. There are times when children cannot get outside for various reasons, and video games can be a good alternative.

The Importance of Reading

Students are regularly assessed for reading comprehension and language arts skills at school. Tests measure a variety of skills and abilities, including phonemic awareness, alphabetic principle, accuracy and fluency with connected text, reading comprehension, and vocabulary.

Reading is considered the gateway to all learning, so it is critical as a parent or guardian to assist and encourage children to read regardless of reading ability. The most effective way to increase literacy skills and to identify challenges that a student may have is to create a consistent reading routine at home. A reading routine provides the practice a child needs to reinforce and build reading and literacy skills, and also helps children develop their imagination and a true love of reading.

Books in a Digital World

With electronic resources comes a significant amount of "screen time" that children spend with technology, including television, movies, computers, cell phones, and gaming systems. It is important to manage "screen time" and also include time for books. Reading a book helps develop attention spans and allows children to build their imagination without the aid of animated graphics, special effects, and sound that may hinder a child's ability to create these for themselves.

Reading in Summer Fit

Recommended reading times, summer reading lists and templates for book reports are available online at www.summerfitlearning.com. Establish reading goals with your child based on reading ability and desired outcome of your summer reading program.

Stay Physically Active Year Round with Safe Routes to School

The *Summer Fit* workbook series is designed to keep children physically and mentally active during the summer. Daily practice and exercise will help lead to healthy, well-balanced lifestyles while away from school, but it is important to extend your *Summer Fit* experience into the new school year.

Summer Fit actively supports companies and non-profit organizations that seek to enhance the overall physical and social well being of children. A great program to become involved with during the school year is Safe Routes to School, which is a national movement to create safe, convenient, and fun opportunities for children to bicycle and walk to and from school. Your school may already have activities such as walking school buses, bike trains, and traffic safety classes that you can participate in, or you could get a Safe Routes to School program started! *Summer Fit* is proud to partner with the Safe Routes to School National Partnership to provide resources, ideas and information to assist parents and guardians in keeping children moving during the school year while reinforcing the importance of physical activity in education.

Because of Safe Routes to School and the National Partnership, new bike lanes, pathways, sidewalks and street crossings are being built throughout the nation. More than 10,000 schools have already benefitted from the federal Safe Routes to School program and it is already evident that Safe Routes to School is making a difference: one study revealed that schools receiving infrastructure improvements through Safe Routes to School funding saw walking and bicycling increase by as much as 200 percent.

USA Cycling

USA Cycling is the official governing body for all disciplines of competitive cycling in the United States, including road, track, mountain bike, BMX, and cyclecross. USA Cycling's mission is to achieve sustained success in international cycling competition and to grow competitive cycling in America. USA Cycling is interested in promoting active and healthy lifestyles and getting more kids on bikes. Visit **www.usacycling.org** to learn more.

Safe Routes to School efforts can start small with one individual or a small group of concerned parents who simply want to assure that their children have healthy transportation alternatives. These efforts can be one day a week, with parent volunteers leading walking or bicycling groups to school. You and your family can learn more about the Safe Routes to School efforts and connect with other parents, teachers and Safe Routes to School advocates by visiting the **Safe Routes to School National Partnership, www.saferoutespartnership.org**

This website also has helpful trip trackers, educational activities and important information on how to champion Safe Routes to School in your community, state, and nationally.

Walking and Riding

Walking and riding a bike are two of the easiest and best ways to get kids moving. These two activities are not only foundation pieces to a healthy and active lifestyle, but they are also fun and practical! Bike safety and maintenance activities created by Mike and The Bike are available at www.mikeandthebike.com

Healthy Eating and Nutrition

A healthy diet and daily exercise will maximize the likelihood of children growing up healthy and strong. Children are still growing and adding bone mass, so a balanced diet is very important to their overall health. Provide three nutritious meals a day that include fruits and vegetables. Try to limit fast food consumption, and find time to cook more at home where you know the source of your food and how your food is prepared. Provide your child with healthy, well-portioned snacks, and try to keep them from eating too much at a time.

As a rule of thumb, avoid foods and drinks that are high in sugars, fat, or caffeine. Try to provide fruits, vegetables, grains, lean meats, chicken, fish, and low-fat dairy products as part of a healthy meal when possible. Obesity and being overweight, even in children, can significantly increase the risk of heart disease, diabetes, and other chronic illnesses. Creating an active lifestyle this summer that includes healthy eating and exercise will help your child maintain a healthy weight and protect them from certain illnesses throughout the year.

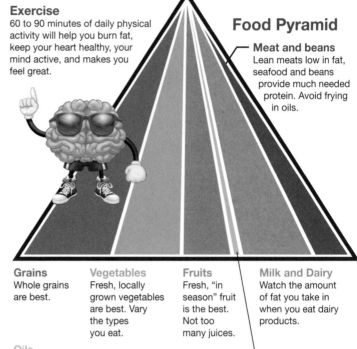

Exercise
60 to 90 minutes of daily physical activity will help you burn fat, keep your heart healthy, your mind active, and makes you feel great.

Food Pyramid

Meat and beans
Lean meats low in fat, seafood and beans provide much needed protein. Avoid frying in oils.

Grains
Whole grains are best.

Vegetables
Fresh, locally grown vegetables are best. Vary the types you eat.

Fruits
Fresh, "in season" fruit is the best. Not too many juices.

Milk and Dairy
Watch the amount of fat you take in when you eat dairy products.

Oils
Oil from fish, nuts and vegetable oil is best. Stay away from saturated and trans fat. Try to stay away from butter, margarine and lard.

Summer Fit actively supports companies and nonprofit organizations that seek to enhance the physical and social well-being of children. Eleanor's Garden is a company that provides valuable resources, ideas, and information to help parents and guardians teach children about the benefits of eating fresh and healthy food by introducing them to the process of growing food. When children have a better understanding of where food comes from and what makes fresh food healthy they are better able to make eating decisions that will keep them fit.

Eleanor's Garden encourages children to learn where food comes from. Children can fuel their curiosity about food including what they like and do not like by getting to know vegetables all the way from planting to harvesting to eating what they grow- nutrition in action! Learn more about how food grows and why it provides the vitamins and nutrients we need to live healthy lifestyles at www.EleanorsGarden.com.

Eleanor's Garden's namesake is Eleanor Roosevelt. As First Lady, she planted the first Victory Garden on the White House grounds, against the wishes of the Department of Agriculture. Mrs. Roosevelt created a fire storm, but by the end of the war 40% of all produce consumed in the United States was raised in backyard gardens.

"It is not fair to ask of others what you are not willing to do yourself."
Eleanor Roosevelt

The Importance of Core Values and Good Character

Teaching your child core values builds good character and gives your child a clear understanding about the kind of behavior you feel is important in your home and in the world. Core values are fundamental to society and are incorporated into our civil laws, but are taught first and foremost at home. Parents and guardians are the most important and influential people in a child's life and should make the conscience decision to raise children who respect and accept themselves, and others around them.

Honesty = Abraham LIncoln

Compassion = Mother Teresa

Trustworthiness = Harriet Tubman

Self-Discipline = Stephanie Lopez Cox

Kindness = Princess Diana

Courage = Rosa Parks

Respect = Gandhi

Responsibility = Terry Fox

Perseverance = Bethany Hamilton

Friendship = Lewis and Clark

Terry Fox

© Photo courtesy of the Terry Fox Foundation

Core Values Activities in *Summer Fit*

Core values activities in *Summer Fit* are a resource for parents and guardians to use in talking about good character. The lessons and activities are designed for parents and guardians to participate with their child. Weekly values and role models correspond from book to book so families with multiple children can discuss the material together and incorporate the activities into daily family life. Remember that children live what they see, so model by example. Talk about and role-play real life situations your child may find him or herself in using the values that are discussed in *Summer Fit*. Help them develop the tools they need to make good choices. *Summer Fit* uses the lives of established world leaders, humanitarians and athletes as positive examples for children to learn from. Discover with your child how and why the qualities these great leaders displayed in difficult times made them great, and how they can display these same qualities at home and in the classroom.

The Foundation for a Better Life

The Foundation for a Better Life began as a simple idea to promote positive values through the belief that the values we live by are worth more when we pass them on. **The Foundation for a Better Life** provides parents, teachers, and children with examples of modern and historic individuals who inspire us through their strong character and examples of how values are displayed in daily life. Visit **www.values.com** for free resources and downloads.

Summer Fit Exercise Program

Daily exercises in *Summer Fit* were created with input from professional trainers, high school and elementary school coaches and physical education instructors. The fitness component was built with the goal of providing parents with enough structure to get children moving and active on a daily basis, but flexible enough so children of all abilities and interests will find exercises and activities interesting. Simply put, *Summer Fit* is designed to get kids moving and having fun.

The workbook-based component is supported by online resources including children's exercise videos, additional exercises and activities to choose from for daily workouts, and informative activity sheets on several topics including: how to fit a bicycle helmet, bike safety, nutrition, bike racing and triathalons.

How the Daily Fitness Program Works

The daily fitness program consists of 2 Aerobic days, 2 Strength days, and 1 Sport day, each represented by a fitness icon. Each day includes a variety of exercises or activities for parents and children to choose from to do together. Children need to warm up each day before they exercise and cool down after they complete their activity or game. Stretching activities are located in the weekly overview.

Children have different abilities and interests, so a variety of exercises, games, and activities are included for each of the three exercise groups.

A Fitness Index is included to create the daily fitness routine. Children are provided with three different exercise options to choose from each day.

After choosing which exercise to do, children determine how long and how many reps they want to do using the provided color chart. Three different levels are offered: beginner, medium and high intensity levels. These levels are suggestions only and can be increased and decreased according to a child's ability and condition. Track fitness results as part of the weekly Incentive Contract to motivate children with rewards and incentives.

Suggested times and reps are included to help create appropriate fitness goals. Keep in mind these are only suggestions and should be increased or decreased at your discretion.

■ 10-30 Seconds or 3-10 Reps

■ 31-60 Seconds or 11-19 Reps

■ 61-90 Seconds or 20-29 Reps

> **Warning: Consult your family doctor prior to starting your child on the Summer Fit fitness program, and remember that the most important thing is to get children moving and have fun.**

FITNESS 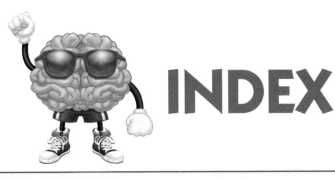 INDEX

The following lists explain how to perform the fitness activities listed in each daily fit exercise. On the Aerobic and Strength days you will be given three exercises to choose from. If you don't know how to perform any of the exercises this list is here to help you. We also provide a list of sports to help you on the sport day, but you may play any sport you choose. For more exercises, sports and other helpful tools go to www.summerfitlearning.com.

Aerobic Exercise = Oxygen

The word "Aerobic" means "needing or giving oxygen." These *Summer Fit* exercises get the heart pumping and oxygen moving to help burn off sugars and calories!

Strength Exercise = Muscle

Strength exercises help make muscles stronger. These *Summer Fit* exercises help build strong muscles to support doing fun activities around the house, school and outdoors!

Play Exercise = Sport Activity

Playing a different sport each week is an opportunity to use the *Summer Fit* oxygen and fitness exercises in a variety of ways. There are a lot of sports to choose from and remember that the most important thing about being *Summer Fit* is to have fun and play!

Aerobic Exercises = Oxygen

Aerobic exercises get you moving. When you move your heart pumps faster and more oxygen gets to your lungs. Movement helps burn off sugars and calories and gets you fit!

Tag: Decide who is "IT." This person will be the one who chases the others. Everybody will get a turn to be "IT!" Choose the boundaries for the game. If a player crosses the boundaries, he or she is automatically "IT." Players should be given a 5-10 second head start to run. The person who is "IT" should count to that number and then start chasing the others. Every other player's objective is to not get tagged. The player who is "IT" tries to touch another player. Once the player succeeds in doing this, the player who has been tagged is now "IT".

Foot Bag (need a hacky sack): Gather players in a circle about four or five feet across. Serve the hacky sack or other foot bag to any player by tossing it gently, about waist high. Keep the foot bag in the air using any part of the body except your arms or hands. Pass the hacky sack back and forth around the circle of players for as long as possible.

Tree Sprints: Find two trees that are 10-12 feet apart. Start with your left leg touching the base of the tree. On "go" sprint as fast as you can to the opposite tree, touch the tree trunk, and sprint back to your start position. Continue sprints until you complete your goal or get tired.

Jumping Jacks: Start by standing with your back straight and knees flexed. Place your arms at your side. Jump in place, raising your hands above your head and clapping while moving your feet apart. Count 1 rep each time you clap your hands. Continue until you reach your goal or get tired.

Aerobic Exercises = Oxygen

Cross-Country Skier: Start in a medium crouch position with one leg in front of the other. Lean forward slightly, keep your knees flexed and bounce in place switching your front foot with your rear foot while swinging your arms back and forth with each bounce. Count 1 rep for each time you reach your start position. Continue until you reach your goal or get tired.

Hide and Seek: Select an area to play tag. Designate a specific area with clear boundaries. Have everyone gather around a tree or other landmark, which is "home base." The child who is "It" must close their eyes and count to 10. Everybody else hides while "It" is counting. "It" calls out, "Ready or not here I come," "It" looks for the other players but be alert because "It" is searching, while the others are trying to run to home base. "It" tries to find and "tag" the players who are hiding before they get to home base. If they get to home base without being tagged they are "safe." The first player who is tagged will be "It" in the next round. If you all get home safely the same child is "It" again!

Turtle and Rabbit: This is a running exercise that you do by running in place. Start in turtle mode by running 25 steps in place very slowly. Then, be a rabbit and run 25 steps as fast as you can!

Wheel Over: Lie down on your back. Raise your legs off the ground and pretend you are riding your bike in the air. Try to keep your back flat on the floor or ground.

Dancing Shoes: Put some music on and dance, dance, dance!

Hill Run or Jog: Find a hill at a park or in your neighborhood. Jog or run up the hill. Pump your arms, keep your back straight, flex your knees, and stay on your toes. Continue for as long as you can or until you reach your time goal.

Run or Jog: Jog or run in your backyard or neighborhood. Pump your arms, keep your back straight, flex your knees, and stay on your toes. Continue for as long as you can or until you reach your time goal.

Ghost Run or Jog: Jog or run in place. Pump your arms, keep your back straight, flex your knees and stay on your toes. Continue for as long as you can or until you reach your time goal.

Ball or Frisbee Toss and Run (need a ball or Frisbee): Start by finding a start place in your backyard or neighborhood park. Toss a ball or Frisbee in front of you 4-6 feet. Walk to pick it up. Toss again 4-6 feet and run medium pace to pick it up. Toss again 4-6 feet and run as fast as you can to pick it up. Repeat as many times as needed to complete your goal or until you are tired. If space is limited, toss back and forth to the same place.

Freeze Tag: In Freeze Tag, one child is "It," and the rest try to keep from getting tagged. When tagged, a child must "freeze" in his tracks until another child unfreezes him (by tagging him or crawling between his legs). When a child is tagged for the third time, he replaces the original "It."

Egg Race (need a spoon and egg): Mark a starting point and a finish point 10-12 feet in distance. Balance an egg on a spoon and race to the finish line! Be careful, don't drop your egg!

Swimming Scissors: Lie down on your stomach. Raise your legs 6-8 inches up and down like scissors cutting through water. Try not to bend your legs and keep your stomach flat on the ground.

Stepping Up: Climb the stairs in your house or apartment. Go slow but see how many you can do!

Hi Yah: Stand with both feet on the ground. When you are ready, kick the air with one leg and scream, "Hi-Yah!" Now do the other leg. "Hi-Yah!"

STRENGTH

Strength Exercises = Muscle

Strength exercises make muscles stronger. When you build strong muscles you are able to lift more, run faster, and do fun activities around your house, school, and outdoors!

Leg Scissors: Lie with your back on the ground. Alternate left to right as you raise your legs 6-8 inches off the ground. Stabilize your body with your arms and raise your chin to your chest. Keep your shoulders off the ground. Repeat with smooth, controlled movements.

Ankle Touches: Lie with your back on the ground. Bend your knees up with your feet flat on the ground. Alternate from left to right touching left hand to left heel and right hand to right heel.

Push-ups: Lie chest-down with your hands at shoulder level, palms flat on the floor, and your feet together. Let yourself down slowly as far as you can go. Straighten your arms and push your body up off the floor. Try not to bend as you push up. Pause for a moment. Then try another one but not too fast.

Moon Touches: Stand with both feet together and back straight. Bend your knees and both of your arms in front of your body. Jump straight up with both feet and reach up as you jump with your left and then your right arm. Repeat with smooth, continuous movement.

Chop and Squat: Place a solid chair with four strong legs behind you. Start by standing in front of the chair with your legs shoulder width apart and slightly flexed. Keep your back upright. Start with your arms raised above your head. As you slowly squat down until you lightly touch the chair behind you, swing your arms between your legs and clap. Raise your arms back above your ahead as you stand up.

Fly in the Ointment: Start by standing straight with your arms stretched out and opened wide. Keep your back upright and slightly bend your knees. Slowly touch one knee to the floor while touching your hands in front of you. Return to starting position and start over by touching the opposite knee to the floor and touching hands in front of you. Complete with smooth, continuous movement.

Jumping Jacks: Stand with your arms at your sides. Be sure your feet are straight and close together. Hold your head straight, but in a comfortable position. Bend your knees and jump up while spreading your arms and legs at the same time. Lift your arms to your ears and open your feet to a little wider than shoulder width. Clap your hands above your head. As you return from jumping up bring your arms back down to your sides and at the same time bring your feet back together.

Jump Rope (need a jump rope): Start by holding an end of the rope in each hand. Position the rope behind you on the ground. Raise your arms up and turn the rope over your head bringing it down in front of you. When it reaches the ground, jump over it. Find a good turning pace, not too slow and not too fast; however you are the most comfortable. Jump over the rope each time it comes around. Continue until you reach your goal or until you get tired.

Hula-Hoop (need a hula-hoop): Start by taking hold of the hula-hoop. Lower it down to about ankle level. Step into it (with both feet). Bring it up to just below your waist. Hold it with both hands and pull it forward so that it is resting against your back. With both hands, fling the hoop to the left so that its inner edge rolls in a circle around your body. Do this a few times so that you get the feel of it. Leave the hula-hoop on the ground for a few minutes and practice your hip movements. Leave your feet firmly planted about shoulder width apart, move your pelvis left, back, right, forward. Do this a few times till you get the feel of it. As you fling the hoop to the left, bring your hips left to meet the hoop and then rotate them back and to the right and forward so that your hips are following the rotation of the hoop. Keep the hoop going around your hips as long as you can. When it falls to the ground pick it up and try again!

Cycling	Walking	Kick Ball	Swimming
Soccer	Rollerblading	Karate	Basketball
Tennis	Four Square	Hopscotch	Frisbee Golf
Badminton	Skating	Football	Baseball

Find What You Like

Everybody has different abilities and interests, so take the time to figure out what activities and exercises you like. Take some time and try them all: soccer, dance, karate, basketball, and skating are only a few. After you have played a lot of different ones, go back and focus on the ones you like! Create your own ways to be active and combine different activities and sports to put your own twist on things. Talk with your parents or caregiver for ideas and have them help you find and do the activities that you like to do. Playing and exercising is a great way to help you become fit, but remember that the most important thing about playing is that you are having fun!

Eat a Variety of Foods, but More Fruits and Vegetables

Lasagna with jelly beans may be your favorite food, but it is best to eat a variety of different foods from all the different food groups. When you eat different foods, you are more likely to get the different nutrients your body needs. Try new foods and mix with old ones you have not tried for a while. Limit your sugar and try to eat more fruits and vegetables with all your meals.

Don't Worry, Be Happy

There seems to be so much going on in the world today that can makes us uneasy. Some of our parents may have lost their jobs. We may have moved away from our friends or from the neighborhood we grew up in. Our classroom or school may have a lot more kids than we are used to being around. Try not to worry about things that you cannot control. Remember that your parents and caregivers love you and your teachers care about you. Remember to smile and be happy, because when you are happy, it's contagious and others around you will be happy too.

Pass on Soda, Hydrate with Water and Milk

It can get hot during the summer, and when you are thirsty, cold water is the best drink around! Water contains no sugar plus it is hands down the most refreshing beverage around! Milk is another great choice. You need calcium to build strong bones, and in addition to making your favorite cereal taste great, milk is a great source of calcium and other nutrients that will help you grow big and strong.

Chill out on Screen Time

Screen time is the amount of time spent watching TV, DVDs or going to the movies, playing video games, texting on the phone and using the computer. The more time you spend looking at a screen the less time you are outside riding your bike, walking, swimming or playing soccer with your friends. Try to spend no more than a couple hours a day in front of a screen for activities other than homework and get outside and play!

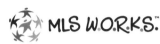

When you complete your incentive contract each week check it off.

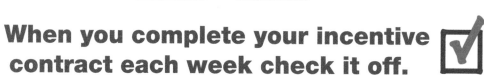

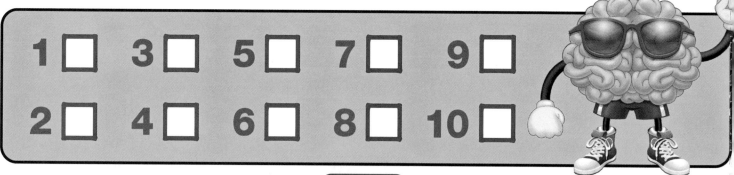

1 □ 3 □ 5 □ 7 □ 9 □

2 □ 4 □ 6 □ 8 □ 10 □

Track your physical progress!
Write down the physical activities you do and the color level you are on each week.

Aerobic	Strength	Level
1		
2		
3		
4		
5		

Aerobic	Strength	Level
6		
7		
8		
9		
10		

This Week We Will Cover

Missing letters, short vowel sounds, healthy choices, long vowel sounds, animals the zoo, addition, subtraction, counting coins, count by 2's, measuring in inches, time, count by 5's, more than, less than, finish the pattern.

Don't Forget to Warm Up

Pick from the aerobic exercises, strength exercises and sport activities this week, but don't forget to warm up. It is always best to prepare your body for any physical activity by moving around and stretching first.

Walk or Jog: Walk or jog for 3-5 minutes to warm up before you exercise. Shake your arms and roll your shoulders when you are finished walking or jogging.

Stretches:

Touch your toes – when standing, bend over at the waist and touch the end of your toes or the floor. Hold this for 10 seconds.

Loose neck – move your head from side to side – trying to touch each shoulder. Now move your head front to back touching your chin to your chest and then looking up and back as far as you can trying to touch your back with the back of your head.

Core Value For the Week
Honesty

Honesty means being fair, truthful, and trustworthy. Honesty means telling the truth no matter what. People who are honest do not lie, cheat, or steal.

Sometimes it is not easy to tell the truth, especially when you are scared and do not want to get in trouble or let others down. Try to remember that even when it is difficult telling the truth is always the best way to handle any situation and people will respect you more.

Honesty in Action
I am honest when I...

Am true to myself and do what I know is right.

Tell the truth.

Keep my promises.

Admit my mistakes.

Express my feelings.

"A half truth is a whole lie."
- Yiddish Proverb

INCENTIVE CONTRACT

My incentive for completing this section will be:

_____

Signed (parent or guardian): _____

✔ off each day's exercises

	day 1	day 2	day 3	day 4	day 5
mind	☐	☐	☐	☐	☐
body	☐	☐	☐	☐	☐

values Write down three things you did this week to show your weekly value.

1. _____

2. _____

3. _____

CONGRATULATIONS

You did a terrific job this week!

Parent or Guardian signature: _____

Use the letters in the hooks to complete each word. Draw a line from the picture of the word in the fish to the word and write the letter that completes the word.

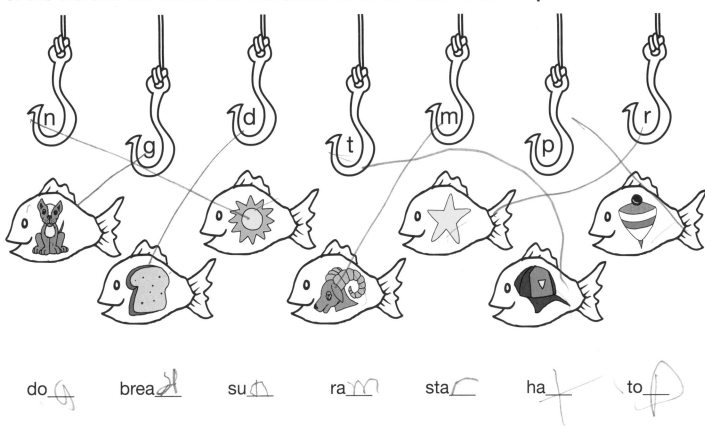

do g   brea d   su n   ra m   sta r   ha t   to p

"a," "e," "i," "o," and "u" are vowels. When vowels are between two consonants they usually make a short sound. Circle the vowel you hear in each word.

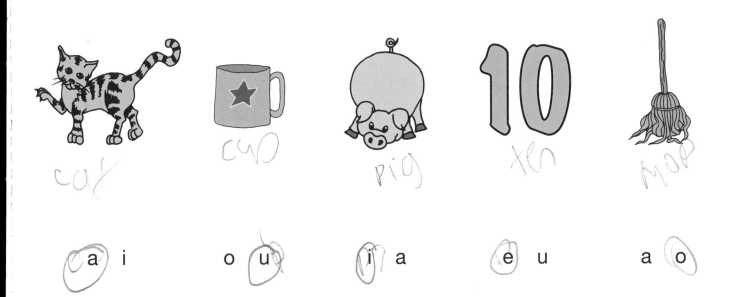

cat   cup   pig   ten   mop

a i   o u   i a   e u   a o

GET FIT TIME – HOW LONG CAN YOU LAST?

AEROBIC

Choose Your Exercise and Level
Watch exercise videos at www.summerfitlearning.com.

Tag	Tree Sprints	Cross Country Skier
10-30 Seconds	31-60 Seconds	61-90 Seconds

Add or subtract.

4 – 2 = __0__   3 + 5 = __8__   2 - 1 = __1__   6 - 3 = __3__

3 + 3 = __6__   5 - 2 = __3__   4 + 4 = __8__   2 + 8 = __10__

Circle the right amount of coins.

50 cents =

25 cents =

Count by 2s to finish the pattern.

2 __4__ 6 __8__ 10 __12__ 14 __16__ 18 __20__ 22

I can choose to be healthy. Circle the healthy choices.

GET FIT TIME! – HOW MANY REPS CAN YOU DO?

STRENGTH

Choose Your Exercise and Level
Watch exercise videos at www.summerfitlearning.com.

Jump Rope   **Hula-hoop**   **Leg Scissors**

3-10 Reps   11-19 Reps   20-29 Reps

How many inches? Use a ruler to measure each object.

worm (length) _____ inches

grasshopper (length) _____ inches

fly (height) _____ inches

feather (height) _____ inches

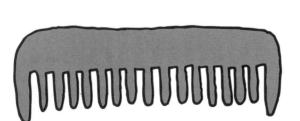

comb (length) _____ inches

Short or long? Long vowel sounds say their name.

apple

cake

Draw a line from each picture to the short worm if it has a short vowel sound or to the long worm if it has a long vowel sound.

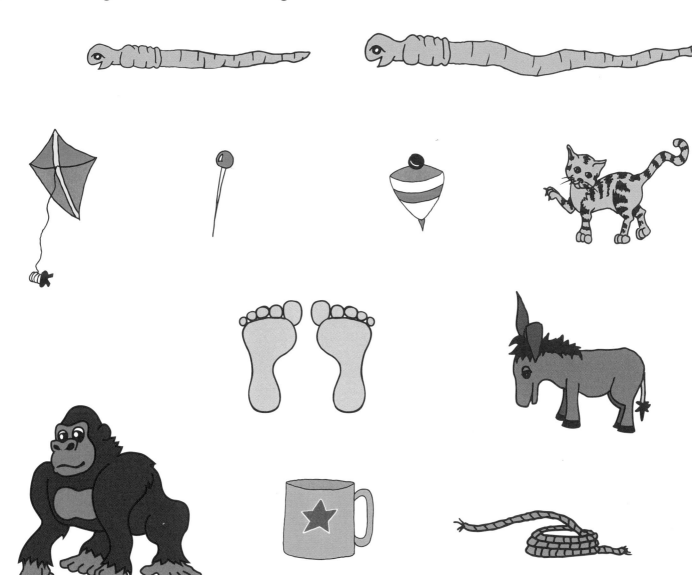

Week 1

Go to www.SummerFitLearning.com for Additional Games, Trivia and Activities!

7

GET FIT TIME – HOW LONG CAN YOU LAST?

AEROBIC

Choose Your Exercise and Level
Watch exercise videos at www.summerfitlearning.com.

Foot Bag   **Jumping Jacks**   **Hide and Seek**

10-30 Seconds   31-60 Seconds   61-90 Seconds

Look at the time. Circle the correct answer.

School starts at 8:00. Sam is…

early.   late.   on time.

Lunch is at 12:00. Sam is…

early.   late.   on time.

Bedtime is 9:00. Sam is…

early.   late.   on time.

Count by 5s

5____15____25____35____45____55____65____75____85____95____

Go to www.SummerFitLearning.com for Additional Games, Trivia and Activities!

Let's go to the zoo.

Going to the zoo is a lot of fun. There are many animals at the zoo, like lions, bears and monkeys. We can see the animals eat and play. Sometimes we can see baby animals. Zookeepers help take care of the animals. The zookeepers give the animals food and keep them clean.

Draw a circle around the correct answer.

Can we see different animals at the zoo?

Yes   No

Can we see lions at the zoo?

Yes   No

Workers that help with the animals are called?

zookeepers   nurses

Underline the right answer.

A zoo is a place to see animals.   A zoo is a place to buy groceries.

Draw a picture of your favorite animal to see at the zoo.

Week 1

Go to www.SummerFitLearning.com for Additional Games, Trivia and Activities!

9

GET FIT TIME! – HOW MANY REPS CAN YOU DO?

STRENGTH

Choose Your Exercise and Level
Watch exercise videos at www.summerfitlearning.com.

Fly in The Ointment

3-10 Reps

Jumping Jacks

11-19 Reps

Jump Rope

20-29 Reps

More than, less than.

6   is more than   4

2   is less than   5

Draw hungry alligators eating more.
They always eat the bigger number.

3      9

7   5

11   >   10

0   1

15   20

10   3

Finish the pattern.

_____,_____,_____,_____

Go to www.SummerFitLearning.com for Additional Games, Trivia and Activities!

HONESTY

Honesty means telling the truth even when it is difficult.

Abraham Lincoln

Abraham Lincoln was so honest that he was given the nickname "Honest Abe." He was taught to tell the truth when he was young and he displayed honesty in the many jobs he did throughout his life including being President of the United States of America. People trusted Lincoln when he told them something. Lincoln knew that it was important to keep his promises and his actions always matched his words, even when it was difficult.

Circle each honest choice and cross out the dishonest one.

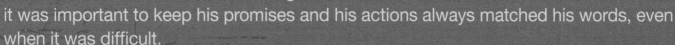

You break your mom's favorite vase so you...	
hide it.	tell her what happened.
You find a $10 bill on the ground at the library so you...	
turn it in to the librarian.	put it in your pocket.
You tell your mom you will clean your room then you....	
play video games.	clean your room.

GET FIT TIME – PLAY A SPORT

SPORT

Choose a Sport to Play

Use the sport index or www.summerfitlearning.com to choose a sport to play.

Try different sports. You can play with your family, friends, or by yourself. Have fun and play with good sportsmanship. Good sportsmanship means that you play fair and treat everyone with respect.

Booklist

The Berenstain Bears Tell the Truth
By Stan and Jan Berenstain

Doctor de Soto
By William Steig

I Did It, I'm Sorry
By Caralyn Buehner

Please visit summerfitlearning.com to download fun summer book report activity sheets.

Honesty Activities

Sign the honesty pledge and have everyone in your family do the same. Draw a picture of how you feel when you tell the truth. Draw a picture of how you feel when you tell a lie. When you tell a lie, you have to tell more lies to cover up for the first one. A lie is like a big, hairy monster that keeps on growing. Telling a lie can feel like a monster is sitting on your chest. Draw a big, hairy, mean monster, then draw a line through it. Hang it up in your room to remind you how bad not telling the truth feels.

Let's Talk About It

Praise your child for telling the truth. Make sure you thank them for telling the truth. Read books on honesty and point out opportunities for honesty. Help your child understand that even half-truths are lies. Setting a good example of honesty is the best lesson a child can get.

Honesty Pledge:

Honest, honest I will be, truthful and sincere.
I'll tell the truth, I will not lie, I will never cheat or steal.
I will admit when I am wrong and promise to be...
Honest in all I say and do and happy to be me.

Sign _____

This Week We Will Cover

Nouns, lifecycle of a butterfly, contractions, missing vowels, days of the week, divide in half, count by 3s, counting coins, doubles, draw half, count by 10s, subtracting tens, time, cardinal numbers.

Don't Forget to Warm Up

Pick from the aerobic exercises, strength exercises and sport activities this week, but don't forget to warm up. It is always best to prepare your body for any physical activity by moving around and stretching first.

Walk or Jog: Walk or jog for 3-5 minutes to warm up before you exercise. Shake your arms and roll your shoulders when you are finished walking or jogging.

Standing Side Stretch: Stretch your right arm all the way up and over to your left side. Curve your body while you do this, so you'll be looking sideways. Hold it by counting all the way to 10. Then do the same thing with the left arm. Remember to count all the way to 10 before you let go.

Sky Stretch: Reach both hands up very-very high! Try to reach so high that you touch the sky! Next, reach all the way down, down, down all the way to your toes. Try to keep your legs straight when you touch your toes. Let's hold this for 10 counts.

Core Value For the Week
COMPASSION

Compassion is caring about the feelings and needs of others.

Sometimes we are so focused on our own feelings that we don't care how other people feel. If we consider other's feelings before our own the world can be a much kinder place. Take time to do something nice for another person and you will feel better about yourself.

Compassion in Action
I am showing compassion when I...

Am kind to people and animals.

Stand up for others.

Care about the earth.

Care when someone is hurt or sad.

Say I'm sorry.

"Repay kindness with kindness." - Aesop

INCENTIVE CONTRACT

My incentive for completing this section will be:

_____

Signed (parent or guardian): _____

✓ off each day's exercises

	day 1	day 2	day 3	day 4	day 5
mind	☐	☐	☐	☐	☐
body	☐	☐	☐	☐	☐

values

Write down three things you did this week to show your weekly value.

1. _____

2. _____

3. _____

CONGRATULATIONS

You did a terrific job this week!

Parent or Guardian signature: _____

A noun is a person, place or thing. Circle the nouns in each house.

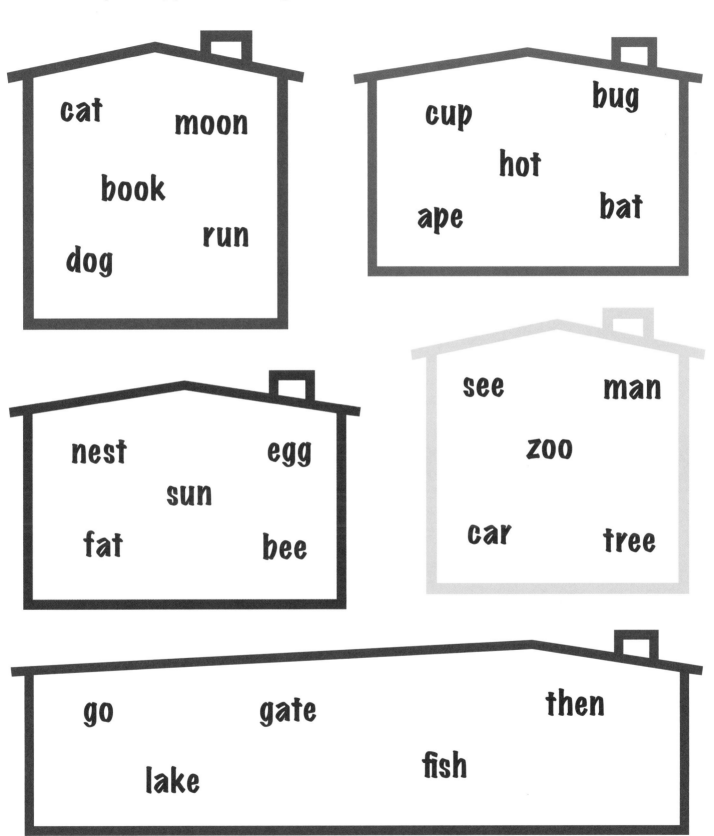

House 1: cat, moon, book, run, dog

House 2: cup, bug, hot, ape, bat

House 3: nest, egg, sun, fat, bee

House 4: see, man, zoo, car, tree

House 5: go, gate, then, lake, fish

Go to www.SummerFitLearning.com for Additional Games, Trivia and Activities!

Day 1

GET FIT TIME – HOW LONG CAN YOU LAST?

AEROBIC

Choose Your Exercise and Level
Watch exercise videos at www.summerfitlearning.com.

Turtle and Rabbit

Dancing Shoes

Run or Jog

10-30 Seconds ☐   31-60 Seconds ☐   61-90 Seconds ☐

When you divide something in half, you divide it into 2 equal parts.
Color half of each group.

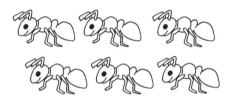 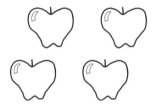 

 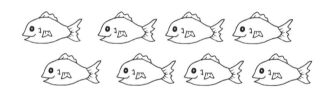 

Count by 3s

3_____9_____15_____21_____27_____

How many cents?

_____cents

Life Cycle of a Butterfly

The life cycle of a butterfly has 4 stages: egg, larva, pupa and butterfly. The adult female lays an egg on a leaf. Out of the egg hatches a caterpillar (larva). The caterpillar eats and eats and gets very large. When the caterpillar is done eating it finds a branch or twig and attaches itself. The caterpillar forms a hard shell called a pupa or chrysalis. While in the pupa the caterpillar changes into a butterfly.

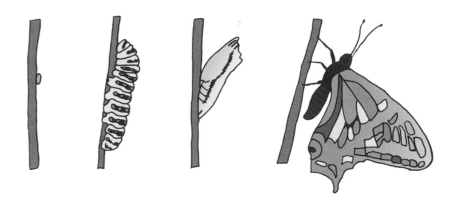

Draw the 4 stages of a butterfly's life cycle.

Larva

Egg

Pupa

Butterfly

Go to www.SummerFitLearning.com for Additional Games, Trivia and Activities!

GET FIT TIME! – HOW MANY REPS CAN YOU DO?

STRENGTH

Choose Your Exercise and Level
Watch exercise videos at www.summerfitlearning.com.

Jumping Jacks   **Ankle Touches**   **Hula-hoop**

3-10 Reps   11-19 Reps   20-29 Reps

Doubles.

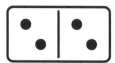   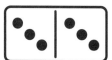   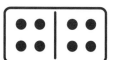

$2 + 2 = 4$ ___ + ___ =   ___ + ___ =

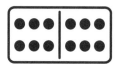      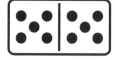

___ + ___ =   ___ + ___ =   ___ + ___ =

Draw the other half of each object.

Draw a line to match the words to the contractions.

Do not

Cannot

She is

It is

He is

We are

They will

I have

Will not

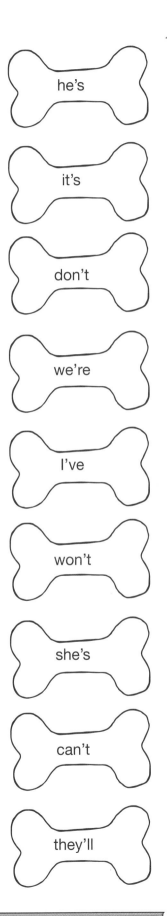

he's

it's

don't

we're

I've

won't

she's

can't

they'll

Go to www.SummerFitLearning.com for Additional Games, Trivia and Activities!

GET FIT TIME – HOW LONG CAN YOU LAST?

AEROBIC

Choose Your Exercise and Level
Watch exercise videos at www.summerfitlearning.com.

Wheel Over   **Hill Run or Jog**   **Ball or Frisbee Toss and Run**

10-30 Seconds   31-60 Seconds   61-90 Seconds

Adding and subtracting 10s.

2 tens + 2 tens	6 tens -4 tens	4 tens + 1 ten	5 tens -2 tens
_____	_____	_____	_____

Solve each problem.

Jill had 50 cents; she spent 20 cents. How much does Jill have left?

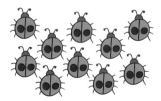   

50 – 20 = _____

Bill found 10 bugs. Then he found 10 more. How many bugs did Bill find?

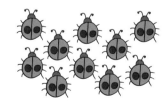

10 + 10 = _____

Go to www.SummerFitLearning.com for Additional Games, Trivia and Activities!

Day 4

Fill in the missing vowels to complete the words. a e i o u

    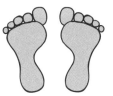

c__ke   m_le   k_te   r__pe   f_et

  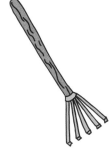

c__be   b_ke   r_ke   b_e   n_te

Write the days of the week and draw a line to the abbreviation.

Sunday   Monday   Tuesday   Wednesday   Thursday   Friday   Saturday

_____	Fri.
_____	Sun.
_____	Sat.
_____	Mon.
_____	Tues.
_____	Thurs.
_____	Wed.

Week 2

Go to www.SummerFitLearning.com for Additional Games, Trivia and Activities!

21

GET FIT TIME! – HOW MANY REPS CAN YOU DO?

STRENGTH

Choose Your Exercise and Level
Watch exercise videos at www.summerfitlearning.com.

Moon Touches

Chop and Squat

Fly in The Ointment

3-10 Reps ☐

11-19 Reps ☐

20-29 Reps ☐

Write the time.

___:___   ___:___   ___:___   ___:___

___:___   ___:___   ___:___   ___:___

first   second   third   fourth   fifth   sixth   seventh   eighth   ninth   tenth

Color the second star yellow.

Circle the eighth star.

Underline the fourth star.

Cross out the seventh star.

Color the tenth star red.

Go to www.SummerFitLearning.com for Additional Games, Trivia and Activities!

Compassion is caring about the feelings and needs of others.

Mother Teresa

Mother Teresa helped many sick and poor people in India. She took care of people who had nobody else to care for them and gave them safety and a place to live. Mother Teresa sacrificed everything so she could help others and her actions inspired other people to give to the poor. Mother Teresa won the Nobel Peace Prize for helping people that nobody else wanted to help.

Use these words to fill in the blank.

compassion   poor   others   cared

Mother Teresa showed_____.

Mother Teresa fed the _____.

The Golden Rule says to treat _____the way you want to be treated.

Mother Teresa _____about everyone.

Week 2

Go to www.SummerFitLearning.com for Additional Games, Trivia and Activities!

23

GET FIT TIME – PLAY A SPORT

SPORT

Choose a Sport to Play

Use the sport index or www.summerfitlearning.com to choose a sport to play.

Try different sports. You can play with your family, friends, or by yourself. Have fun and play with good sportsmanship. Good sportsmanship means that you play fair and treat everyone with respect.

Booklist

Arnie and the New Kid
By Nancy Carlson

The Kissing Hand
By Audrey Penn

Hooway for Wadney Wat
By Helen Lester

Please visit summerfitlearning.com to download fun summer book report activity sheets.

Compassion Activities

Collect food from family, friends and neighbors to donate to a food bank.

Make a card for someone who is sick or lonely.

Go on a "Garbage Walk" collecting litter in your neighborhood or community.

Let's Talk About It

Any child has the potential to change the world. Help your child find his/her gifts and encourage them to use those gifts to help others. Volunteer as a family and make it a regular part of your family's life. This way your child experiences concrete ways they can help others and make a difference.

This Week We Will Cover

Verbs, alphabet writing, alphabetical order, synonyms, ordering a story, fourths, greater than, less than, shapes, counting by 10's, calendar days, tally marks, adding three numbers.

Don't Forget to Warm Up

Pick from the aerobic exercises, strength exercises and sport activities this week but don't forget to warm up. It is always best to prepare your body for any physical activity by moving around and stretching first.

Walk or Jog: Walk or jog for 3-5 minutes to warm up before you exercise. Shake your arms and roll your shoulders when you are finished walking or jogging.

"V" Stretch: Sit on the ground with your legs out in front of you making a letter "V" shape. Reach for your toes again and count to 8 this time.

Neck stretch: While sitting or standing with your head in its normal upright position, slowly tilt it to the right until tension is felt on the left side of your neck. Hold that tension for 10 to 30 seconds and then return your head to the upright position.

Repeat to the left side, and then toward the front. Always return to the upright position before moving on.

Core Value For the Week
TRUSTWORTHINESS

Trustworthiness is being worthy of trust. It means people can count on you. You are honest and you keep your word.

Sometimes it is easy to forget what we tell people because we try to do so much or we are constantly moving around. Try to slow down and follow through on what you say before moving onto something else.

Trust in Action
I am being trustworthy when I...

Am honest.

Keep my promises.

Finish what I start.

Am a good friend.

Have the courage to do the right thing.

"Trust people and they will be true to you."
- Ralph Waldo Emerson

INCENTIVE CONTRACT

My incentive for completing this section will be:

_____

Signed (parent or guardian): _____

✓ off each day's exercises

	day 1	day 2	day 3	day 4	day 5
mind	☐	☐	☐	☐	☐
body	☐	☐	☐	☐	☐

values Write down three things you did this week to show your weekly value.

1. _____

2. _____

3. _____

CONGRATULATIONS

You did a terrific job this week!

Parent or Guardian signature: _____

Verbs are words that tell what something or someone does. They are "action words."

"The shark <u>swims</u>."

Circle the verbs.

run	blue	see	hide	play	dog
swim	sleep	girl	sun	smell	fly

Use the verbs above to finish the sentences.

I like to _____ outside.

I _____ the cookies baking.

I _____ in my bed.

I will _____ my kite.

I play _____ and seek.

GET FIT TIME – HOW LONG CAN YOU LAST?

AEROBIC

Choose Your Exercise and Level
Watch exercise videos at www.summerfitlearning.com.

Freeze Tag   **Swimming Scissors**   **Hi-Yah**

10-30 Seconds ☐   31-60 Seconds ☐   61-90 Seconds ☐

Color 1/4.

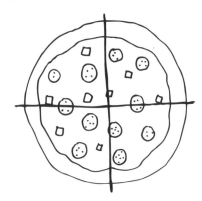 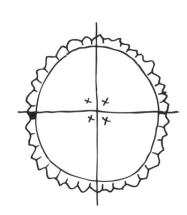 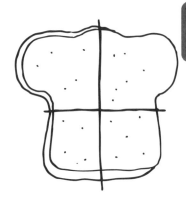

Write the number that is one more.

25 _____   13 _____   36 _____   9 _____

Write >, <, or =

22 _____ 28   15 _____ 10   36 _____ 63

10 _____ 10   50 _____ 40   18 _____ 18

Write the alphabet in your nicest handwriting.

Aa Bb Cc Dd Ee Ff Gg Hh Ii

Jj Kk Ll Mm Nn Oo Pp Qq Rr

Ss Tt Uu Vv Ww Xx Yy Zz

Write the words in alphabetical order.

cat _____   man _____

fat _____   tan _____

bat _____   fan _____

at _____   pan _____

rat _____   ran _____

GET FIT TIME! – HOW MANY REPS CAN YOU DO?

STRENGTH

Choose Your Exercise and Level
Watch exercise videos at www.summerfitlearning.com.

Push-ups	Moon Touches	Chop and Squat
3-10 Reps	11-19 Reps	20-29 Reps

Circle the shape that matches the word.

Oval

Triangle

Rectangle

Square

1 ten = ___ cents   4 tens = ___ cents   7 tens = ___ cents

2 tens = ___ cents   5 tens = ___ cents   8 tens = ___ cents

3 tens = ___ cents   6 tens = ___ cents   9 tens = ___ cents

Calendar days.

January	31	July	31
February	28	August	31
March	31	September	30
April	30	October	31
May	31	November	30
June	30	December	31

Thirty days has September, April, June, and November.
All the rest have 31. Except February, which has only 28.

_____is the first month of the year.

The shortest month is_____.

_____ is the last month of the year.

How many days does April have?_____

What month is your birthday in?_____

GET FIT TIME – HOW LONG CAN YOU LAST?

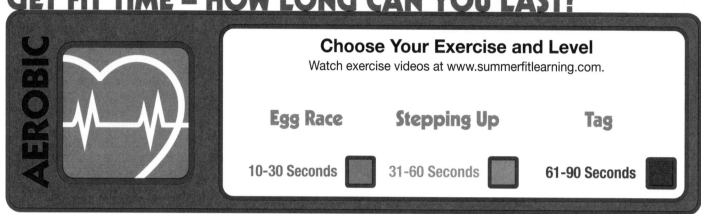

AEROBIC

Choose Your Exercise and Level
Watch exercise videos at www.summerfitlearning.com.

Egg Race	Stepping Up	Tag
10-30 Seconds ☐	31-60 Seconds ☐	61-90 Seconds ☐

Synonyms are words that mean the same thing.
Draw a line to match the synonyms.

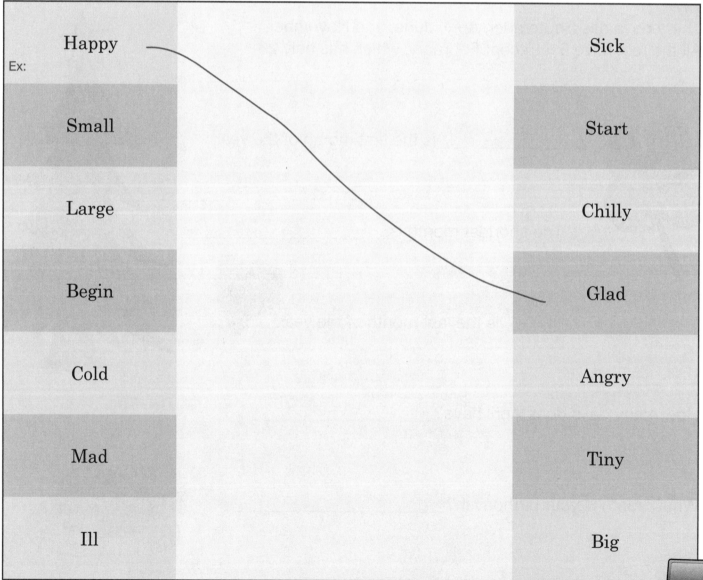

Ex: Happy	Sick
Small	Start
Large	Chilly
Begin	Glad
Cold	Angry
Mad	Tiny
Ill	Big

Number the parts of the stories in the correct order.

The bird built its nest. Then the bird laid 3 eggs in the nest. After a while the eggs hatched and the baby birds were hungry. The mother bird fed her babies.

_____   _____   _____   _____

Mary and her mother wanted to make a cake. First they got the ingredients they would need. They followed the recipe to make the batter. Mary's mother put the cake in the oven to bake. After an hour the cake was done. That night Mary's family had a birthday party and served the cake. It was delicious!

_____   _____   _____   _____

GET FIT TIME! – HOW MANY REPS CAN YOU DO?

STRENGTH

Choose Your Exercise and Level
Watch exercise videos at www.summerfitlearning.com.

Jumping Jacks   **Jump Rope**   **Hula-hoop**

3-10 Reps ☐   11-19 Reps ☐   20-29 Reps ☐

Count by 5s to 100.

5	10	

_____   _____   _____   _____   _____

_____   _____   _____   _____   _____

_____   _____   _____   _____   _____

Add.

```
  2        4        5        3        1
  3        2        1        3        2
 +1       +2       +2       +3       +5
____     ____     ____     ____     ____
```

Day 4

34

TRUSTWORTHINESS

Being Trustworthy means doing what you promise, even when it is difficult.

Harriet Tubman

Harriet Tubman was a slave before the Civil War. She had to work very hard with no pay and was sometimes treated very badly. From the time she was a little girl, Harriet dreamed of freedom and although she was small, she was strong-willed. When she was an adult, Harriet escaped slavery to become free, and she wanted to help others be free. She risked her life many times to lead other slaves to safety and freedom. People trusted her with their lives and she never let them down.

Draw a picture of one way you can be trustworthy at home.

Week 3   35

Go to www.SummerFitLearning.com for Additional Games, Trivia and Activities!

GET FIT TIME – PLAY A SPORT

SPORT

Choose a Sport to Play

Use the sport index or www.summerfitlearning.com to choose a sport to play.

Try different sports. You can play with your family, friends, or by yourself. Have fun and play with good sportsmanship. Good sportsmanship means that you play fair and treat everyone with respect.

Booklist

Abraham Lincoln
By Ingri and Edgar Parin D'Aulaire

My Brother the Thief
By Marlene Fanta Shyer

The Bad Times of Irma Baumlein
By Carol Brink

Please visit summerfitlearning.com to download fun summer book report activity sheets.

Trustworthy Activities

Being trustworthy means being honest with the words we say and the things we do. Cut several strips of paper. On each piece write one way you can show trustworthiness. Glue them together to make a chain. Each day take one "loop" off to and do what is written.

Play a game of trust with a friend or family member. Wear a blindfold and let the other one lead you around the house, in the yard, or around the neighborhood. How hard is it to completely trust someone?

Let's Talk About It

Help your child understand that it is important to be honest because it makes you trustworthy later on. Once you have been dishonest it is hard for people to trust you. Discuss the story "Peter and the Wolf."

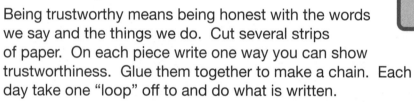

Stepping Stones

Stepping Stones Entertainment™ was founded by parents who wanted to provide meaningful family movies to help inspire common values. It is made up of people from many different backgrounds, nationalities and beliefs. For more than 20 years, Stepping Stones has provided families with movies about integrity, charity, forgiveness and many other common values through hundreds of films for all ages. Learn more at **www.steppingstones.com**.

36

Go to www.SummerFitLearning.com for Additional Games, Trivia and Activities!

This Week We Will Cover

Singular, plural, asking and telling sentences, adjectives, compound words, tens and ones, following directions, larger and smaller numbers, thirds, finish the pattern, pet table, fact families, sums, doubles.

Don't Forget to Warm Up

Pick from the aerobic exercises, strength exercises and sport activities this week but don't forget to warm up. It is always best to prepare your body for any physical activity by moving around and stretching first.

Walk or Jog: Walk or jog for 3-5 minutes to warm up before you exercise. Shake your arms and roll your shoulders when you are finished walking or jogging.

Reach to the sky: Stand with feet shoulder-width apart. Raise both arms overhead so that your hands are intertwined with palms together. Hold for 10 to 30 seconds and relax.

Calf stretch: Place your hands against a wall while standing upright. Bend one knee slightly in front of your body while you extend the opposite leg backward until the foot is placed flat on the floor. With your back straight, you should feel some tension in the back of your leg. Hold the stretch for 15 to 20 seconds and repeat twice with each leg.

Core Value For the Week
SELF-DISCIPLINE

Self-discipline means self-control. It is working hard and getting yourself to do what is important.

It is easy to loose interest in what we are doing, especially if it does not come fast and easy. Focus your attention on what you are trying to accomplish and try to block out other things until you reach your goal.

Self-Discipline in Action
I am practicing self-discipline when I...

Keep my hands to myself.

Keep control of myself and my emotions.

Work hard and do my best.

Use my time wisely.

"Those who command themselves will command others."
- William Hazlit

INCENTIVE CONTRACT

My incentive for completing this section will be:

_____

Signed (parent or guardian): _____

✓ off each day's exercises

	day 1	day 2	day 3	day 4	day 5
mind	☐	☐	☐	☐	☐
body	☐	☐	☐	☐	☐

values

Write down three things you did this week to show your weekly value.

1. _____

2. _____

3. _____

CONGRATULATIONS

You did a terrific job this week!

Parent or Guardian signature: _____

Plurals are words that mean more than one. Plurals are made by adding "s" or "es."

Read the plural words. Write the singular form.

cars _____   balls _____

boxes _____   trucks _____

shirts _____   foxes _____

girls _____   dresses _____

When words end with a "y," we change the "y" to an "i" and add "es."
Cross out the "y" and add "ies." Write the new word.

baby _____

bunny _____

story _____

guppy _____

Week 4

39

Go to www.SummerFitLearning.com for Additional Games, Trivia and Activities!

GET FIT TIME – HOW LONG CAN YOU LAST?

AEROBIC

Choose Your Exercise and Level
Watch exercise videos at www.summerfitlearning.com.

Foot Bag	Tree Sprints	Jumping Jacks
10-30 Seconds	31-60 Seconds	61-90 Seconds

Using tens and ones, find the total value.

1 ten 0 ones = 10

1 ten + 1 one = 11

____ ten ____ones = _____

____ ten ____ones = _____

____ ten ____ones = _____

____ ten ____ones = _____

____ tens ____ones = _____

____ tens ____ones = _____

____ tens ____ones = _____

____ tens ____ones = _____

____ tens ____ones = _____

Go to www.SummerFitLearning.com for Additional Games, Trivia and Activities!

Asking and telling sentences.

Change each asking sentence to a telling sentence.

What is the dog playing with?

_____

Is it cold or warm today?

_____

Who is riding the bike?

_____

Telling sentences end in a period [.]. Asking sentences end in a question mark [?]. Add the correct punctuation mark to each sentence.

Are you going to swim _____

My fish is orange _____

Are the birds in the tree _____

She is baking a cake _____

Go to www.SummerFitLearning.com for Additional Games, Trivia and Activities!

GET FIT TIME! – HOW MANY REPS CAN YOU DO?

STRENGTH

Choose Your Exercise and Level
Watch exercise videos at www.summerfitlearning.com.

Leg Scissors	Ankle Touches	Push-ups
3-10 Reps	11-19 Reps	20-29 Reps

Circle the larger number. Underline the smaller number.

24 28	31 29	45 40
13 11	8 10	10 20
50 51	23 32	15 12

Color 1/3.

  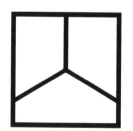 

Finish the pattern.

5 _____ 15 _____ 25 _____ 35 _____ 45 _____ 55 _____ 65

Adjectives are words that describe a noun. Circle the adjectives.

Red dog

Blue bird

Slimy worm

Fast dog

Soft cat

Tiny bug

Hot day

Think of an adjective to describe each noun.

_____ fish

_____ boy

_____ book

_____ frog

_____ lake

_____ cup

GET FIT TIME – HOW LONG CAN YOU LAST?

AEROBIC

Choose Your Exercise and Level
Watch exercise videos at www.summerfitlearning.com.

Cross Country Skier	Hide and Seek	Turtle and Rabbit
10-30 Seconds	31-60 Seconds	61-90 Seconds

This table shows all the pets of the children in Mrs. Bell's class. Count how many of each pet.

Dogs   _____

Cats   _____

Penguins   _____

Fish   _____

Hermit crabs _____

Grasshoppers _____

Rams   _____

Which pet is most popular? _____

How many more dogs are there than crabs? _____

Which pet lives in water? _____

Which pet is there only 1 of? _____

Compound words are bigger words made by two smaller words put together. Add the smaller words together to make a compound word. Write the new word.

Bird + house = _____

Snow + man = _____

Foot + ball = _____

Hay + stack = _____

Fire + man = _____

Air + plane = _____

Cup + cake = _____

Day 4

GET FIT TIME! – HOW MANY REPS CAN YOU DO?

STRENGTH

Choose Your Exercise and Level
Watch exercise videos at www.summerfitlearning.com.

Leg Scissors	**Ankle Touches**	**Push-ups**
3-10 Reps	11-19 Reps	20-29 Reps

Fact families.

4 + 3 = _____   3 + 4 = _____   2 + 6 = _____   6 + 2 = _____

7 - 4 = _____   7 - 3 = _____   8 - _____ = 2   8 - _____ = 6

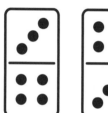 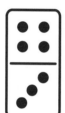 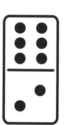 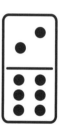

Ex: Double 4 = __8__   Double 3 = _____

Double 2 = _____   Double 5 = _____

Double 6 = _____   Double 7 = _____

  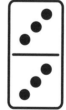 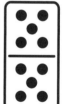 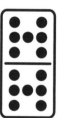

Go to www.SummerFitLearning.com for Additional Games, Trivia and Activities!

Self-discipline is to have control of your actions and to enable you to achieve your goals.

Stephanie Lopez Cox works hard to reach her goals. Her focus and dedication helped her gain a spot on the U.S. National Women's Soccer Team that won gold in the Olympics. Stephanie practices very hard and is committed to doing things that will help her be the best athlete she can be. Stephanie is dedicated to bettering the world around her, and is committed to helping children in foster care because she grew up with foster siblings.

Photo courtesy of Stephanie Lopez Cox

Stephanie practices hard to be the best soccer player she can be. She also works hard to be the best person she can be by helping others. Write down what Stephanie does to help others. Draw a picture.

Week 4

Go to www.SummerFitLearning.com for Additional Games, Trivia and Activities!

47

GET FIT TIME – PLAY A SPORT

SPORT

Choose a Sport to Play

Use the sport index or www.summerfitlearning.com to choose a sport to play.

Try different sports. You can play with your family, friends, or by yourself. Have fun and play with good sportsmanship. Good sportsmanship means that you play fair and treat everyone with respect.

Booklist

Greedy Greeny
By Jack Gantos

A Chair for my Mother
By Vera B. Williams

Oh, the Places You'll Go!
By Dr. Seuss

Please visit summerfitlearning.com to download fun summer book report activity sheets.

Self-Discipline Activities

As a family decide on something special you want to save for, make a plan to save money, and practice self-discipline to achieve your goal.

Make a daily schedule for yourself. Hang it up and follow it. Include exercise, hygiene and cleaning your room. Give up sweets for a week. Make a list of healthy snacks you can eat instead. Practice self-discipline and stick to it!

Let's Talk About It

Discuss healthy choices in diet and exercise with your child. Talk about what happens to us when we do not practice self-discipline in taking care of our bodies. Set a good example by making healthful living a priority in your family.

This Week We Will Cover

The ant, capitalization, exclamatory sentences, antonyms, missing letters "oa" and "ee," long "e," numbers 51-100, units of measurement, sides and corners, 1/2, 1/3, 1/4, shapes, greater than, less than, equal to, word problems, tens and ones.

Don't Forget to Warm Up

Pick from the aerobic exercises, strength exercises and sport activities this week, but don't forget to warm up. It is always best to prepare your body for any physical activity by moving around and stretching first.

Walk or Jog: Walk or jog for 3-5 minutes to warm up before you exercise. Shake your arms and roll your shoulders when you are finished walking or jogging.

Knee to chest: Lie on your back on a mat with your legs straight. Bend your left knee, and bring it up toward your chest. Grasp the underside of your thigh, and slowly pull your thigh to your chest. Hold for 10 to 30 seconds. Release, and repeat with the right leg.

Sky Stretch: Reach both hands up very, very high! Try to reach so high that you touch the sky! Next, reach all the way down, down, down all the way to your toes. Try to keep your legs straight when you touch your toes. Let's hold this for 10 counts.

Core Value For the Week
KINDNESS

Kindness is caring about people, animals, and the earth. It is looking for ways to help others.

Being nice to others catches on and when people are nice to each other people feel better about themselves and others. Small things make a big difference so when you smile, lend a helping hand and show concern for others you are making the world a better place.

Kindness in Action
I am being kind when I...

Look for ways to help others.

Take good care of people, animals and the earth.

Accept people who are different.

Comfort someone who is sad.

Speak kindly.

"Kindness is the language which the deaf can hear and the blind can see."
- Mark Twain

INCENTIVE CONTRACT

My incentive for completing this section will be:

_____

Signed (parent or guardian): _____

✓ off each day's exercises

	day 1	day 2	day 3	day 4	day 5
mind	☐	☐	☐	☐	☐
body	☐	☐	☐	☐	☐

values

Write down three things you did this week to show your weekly value.

1. _____

2. _____

3. _____

CONGRATULATIONS

You did a terrific job this week!

Parent or Guardian signature: _____

An ant is an insect. It has six legs and a three-part body. Ants use their antennae to find food. They smell and feel with their antennae. Ants live and work together in a colony. Every colony has a queen. The queen's job is to lay the eggs. The other ants are worker ants, nursery ants, and soldier ants.

In an anthill there are many rooms and tunnels, all made by the busy ants. Some rooms are used to store food, while other rooms are used for eggs and ants that have just hatched. Ants are very strong and can carry up to 50 times their weight.

Label the parts of the ant.

head
abdomen
thorax
eyes
antennae
legs

Circle the correct answer.

The eggs are laid by the _____.	queen	soldier ants
Ants are _____.	weak	strong
What do ants use to find food?	ears	antennae
How many legs to ants have?	6	8

Week 5

Go to www.SummerFitLearning.com for Additional Games, Trivia and Activities!

51

GET FIT TIME – HOW LONG CAN YOU LAST?

AEROBIC

Choose Your Exercise and Level
Watch exercise videos at www.summerfitlearning.com.

Wheel Over	Dancing Shoes	Hill Run or Jog
10-30 Seconds	31-60 Seconds	61-90 Seconds

Fill in the numbers from 51 to 100.

51 _____   53 _____   55 _____   57 _____   59 _____

61 _____   63 _____   65 _____   67 _____   69 _____

71 _____   73 _____   75 _____   77 _____   79 _____

81 _____   83 _____   85 _____   87 _____   89 _____

91 _____   93 _____   95 _____   97 _____   99 _____

Circle the unit you would use to measure each object.

How would you measure length?

inches   feet   miles   yard

miles   yards   feet   inches

How would you measure weight?

ounces   pounds   quarts   ounces

pounds   tons   ounces   miles

How would you measure liquid?

quarts   pounds   miles   inches

miles   ounces   pounds   gallons

Go to www.SummerFitLearning.com for Additional Games, Trivia and Activities!

Day 2

Capitalize the first word of every sentence and the word I.
Copy each sentence correctly.

i see the cat on the mat.

_____

the man had a bag of sand.

_____

i can swim all day.

_____

Exclamatory sentences show strong feelings and end with exclamation marks. Circle the exclamation mark in each sentence.

Help! The snake is out!   **Oh no! I broke the glass!**

Get the dog!   **Ow! That pot is hot!**

Wow! That cat is fast!   **Look out!**

Week 5   53
Go to www.SummerFitLearning.com for Additional Games, Trivia and Activities!

GET FIT TIME! – HOW MANY REPS CAN YOU DO?

STRENGTH

Choose Your Exercise and Level
Watch exercise videos at www.summerfitlearning.com.

Fly in The Ointment

3-10 Reps

Moon Touches

11-19 Reps

Hula-hoop

20-29 Reps

How many sides and corners?

____sides____corners

____sides____corners

____sides____corners

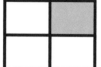

____sides____corners

Label each part: 1/2   1/3   1/4.

 _____

 _____

 _____

 _____

 _____

_____

How many halves in a whole? _____   How many thirds in a whole? _____

How many fourths in a whole? _____

Antonyms are words that have opposite meanings.
Draw a line to connect the antonyms.

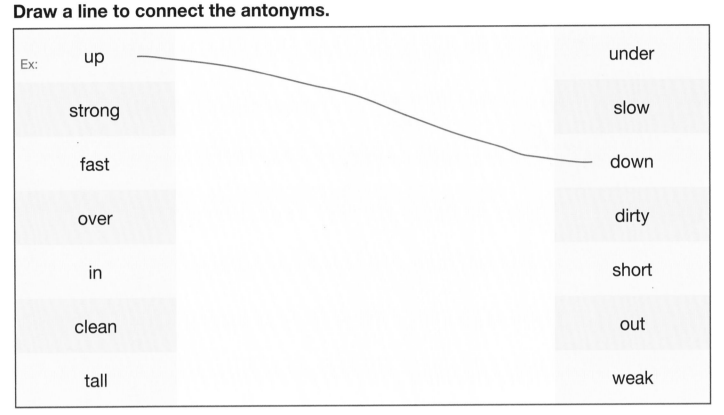

Ex: up   under

strong   slow

fast   down

over   dirty

in   short

clean   out

tall   weak

Color the shapes.

red triangles
blue squares
green rectangles
yellow circles
black ovals

GET FIT TIME – HOW LONG CAN YOU LAST?

AEROBIC

Choose Your Exercise and Level
Watch exercise videos at www.summerfitlearning.com.

Turtle and Rabbit

Wheel Over

Dancing Shoes

10-30 Seconds   31-60 Seconds   61-90 Seconds

Mark >, <, or =.

Ex: 4 + 1 __<__ 5 + 2   3 + 3 _____ 2 + 4   4 + 4 _____ 2 + 1

3 + 4 _____ 2 + 3   9 + 1 _____ 6 + 2   2 + 2 _____ 3 + 1

5 + 5 _____ 7 + 4   8 + 3 _____ 7 + 2   1 + 8 _____ 3 + 3

2 + 7 _____ 6 + 1   1 + 3 _____ 2 + 8   2 + 6 _____ 7 + 2

9 + 5 _____ 7 + 4   6 + 3 _____ 5 + 5   2 + 6 _____ 5 + 1

1 + 1 _____ 3 + 0   7 + 5 _____ 3 + 8   4 + 5 _____ 2 + 6

Fill in the missing letters "oa" or "ee" to complete the word.

 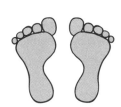  

c_____t   f_____t   b_____t   b_____   s_____p

t_____d   tr_____   r_____d   g_____t   kn_____

Add an "e" at the end of each word to change the short vowel sound to a long vowel sound.

bit + e = _____   kit + e = _____

can + e = _____   man + e = _____

van + e = _____   cap + e = _____

tap + e = _____   mat + e = _____

GET FIT TIME! – HOW MANY REPS CAN YOU DO?

STRENGTH

Choose Your Exercise and Level
Watch exercise videos at www.summerfitlearning.com.

Jumping Jacks	**Jump Rope**	**Hula-hoop**
3-10 Reps ☐	11-19 Reps ☐	20-29 Reps ☐

Problems to solve.

There are 25 flowers

12 more are planted. How many are there now?

$$\begin{array}{r} 25 \\ +\ 12 \\ \hline \text{Ex: } \quad 37 \end{array}$$

There were 32 children at the party.

10 went home. How many are still there? _____

You found 15 shells.

Your brother found 13. How many do you have together? _____

Ann had 60 cents.

She bought an apple for 30 cents. How much does she have left? _____

1 ten and 6 ones = _____   2 tens and 4 ones = _____

3 tens and 5 ones = _____   6 tens and 8 ones = _____

5 tens and 9 ones = _____   4 tens and 4 ones = _____

Go to www.SummerFitLearning.com for Additional Games, Trivia and Activities!

KINDNESS

Kindness is being nice and caring about people, animals, and the earth. Kindness includes looking for ways to help others.

Princess Diana

Princess Diana showed kindness to people from all walks of life. Rich or poor, old or young, it did not matter. She cared for people society had forgotten and made ordinary people feel extraordinary. Princess Diana used her power and fame to give hope to the hopeless by taking time to listen and care. She had a smile for everyone and opened her heart to those in need.

Tell someone they are special

Share your snack

Kindness starts with me

Pick up something someone has dropped

Pick up trash on playground

Call your Grandparents and tell them you love them

Hold the door open for someone

Take garbage out without being asked

Week 5

59

Go to www.SummerFitLearning.com for Additional Games, Trivia and Activities!

GET FIT TIME – PLAY A SPORT

SPORT

Choose a Sport to Play

Use the sport index or www.summerfitlearning.com to choose a sport to play.

Try different sports. You can play with your family, friends, or by yourself. Have fun and play with good sportsmanship. Good sportsmanship means that you play fair and treat everyone with respect.

Booklist

The Kindness Quilt
By Nancy Wallace

Jamaica Tag - Along
By Juanita Havill

**The Elves and
the Shoemaker**
By Paul Galdone

**Please visit
summerfitlearning.com
to download fun
summer book report
activity sheets.**

Kindness Activities

Make a kindness chain. Have your parent help you cut seven strips of paper. Write an act of kindness on each strip. Every morning pull off one strip and do that act of kindness.

Make cards for sick children in the hospital. Have your parents take you to the hospital to deliver them. You will surely make someone smile!

Write a letter or draw a picture for your parents or guardian telling how much you love them.

Let's Talk About It

Help your child understand that random acts of kindness mean acts of kindness that aren't expected. Teach them that kindnesses can be big or small and can be as simple as a smile. Use everyday examples of kindness to show them how easy being kind can be and how much it means to others.

This Week We Will Cover

Long a sounds "ai" and "ay," manners, needs and wants, classifying objects, how much does it cost? Count backwards by 5's, measuring centimeters, largest smallest, finish the pattern, time, temperature, follow directions.

Don't Forget to Warm Up

Pick from the aerobic exercises, strength exercises and sport activities this week, but don't forget to warm up. It is always best to prepare your body for any physical activity by moving around and stretching first.

Walk or Jog: Walk or jog for 3-5 minutes to warm up before you exercise. Shake your arms and roll your shoulders when you are finished walking or jogging.

Wall Stretch: Stand facing a wall. Place your right palm on the wall so it's in line with your shoulder, and point your fingers back. Keep your right hand planted firmly, and bend your left arm behind you. Now walk a few small steps to the left and stop when you feel a good stretch in your right shoulder and chest. Hold for 30 seconds and then walk back towards the wall.

Reach to the sky: Stand with feet shoulder-width apart. Raise both arms overhead so that your hands are intertwined with palms together. Hold for 10 to 30 seconds and relax.

Core Value For the Week COURAGE

Courage means doing the right thing even when it is difficult and you are afraid. It means to be brave.

It can be a lot easier to do the right thing when everybody else is doing it, but it can be a lot harder to do it on our own or when nobody is looking. Remember who you are and stand up for what you believe in when it is easy and even more so when it is hard.

Courage in Action
I am showing courage when I...

Am proud of who I am and believe in myself.

Try new things even though I might fail.

Stand up for what is right even if I stand alone.

Face my fears and try to overcome them.

"You must do the thing you think you cannot do."
– Elenor Roosevelt

INCENTIVE CONTRACT

My incentive for completing this section will be:

_____

Signed (parent or guardian): _____

✓ off each day's exercises

	day 1	day 2	day 3	day 4	day 5
mind	☐	☐	☐	☐	☐
body	☐	☐	☐	☐	☐

values

Write down three things you did this week to show your weekly value.

1. _____

2. _____

3. _____

CONGRATULATIONS

You did a terrific job this week!

Parent or Guardian signature: _____

Add "ai" or "ay" to complete these long "a" words.

p_____nt   d_____   tr_____n   tr_____   r_____n

h_____   ch_____n   r_____   gr_____n   pl_____

Finish each sentence with a word from above.

Dad will _____ the house.

I love to _____ in the _____.

Horses like to eat _____ and _____.

Mom served tea on a fancy _____.

Week 6

63

Go to www.SummerFitLearning.com for Additional Games, Trivia and Activities!

GET FIT TIME – HOW LONG CAN YOU LAST?

AEROBIC

Choose Your Exercise and Level
Watch exercise videos at www.summerfitlearning.com.

Freeze Tag   **Egg Race**   **Swimming Scissors**

10-30 Seconds ☐   31-60 Seconds ☐   61-90 Seconds ☐

How much does it cost?

_____   _____

_____   _____

Count backwards by 5s.

100 _____ 90 _____ 80 _____ 70 _____ 60 _____

50 _____ 40 _____ 30 _____ 20 _____ 10 _____

Go to www.SummerFitLearning.com for Additional Games, Trivia and Activities!

Don't forget your manners!

Good manners are important and help us get along with others. Answer the questions using the words from the list.

please	thank you	hello	may
nice	open	excuse me	sorry

Greet people with a _____ and a smile.

When you meet someone new, you say, "_____ to meet you."

When you make a mistake you say, "I am _____."

Hold the door _____ for people.

It is polite to say "_____," when someone gives you a gift.

Say "_____" when you bump in to someone.

When you ask for something, you should say "_____."

When you ask permission to do something, you say, "_____ I, please?"

Unscramble the letters to make a manners word.

esplae _____   em sxecue _____

oyu htkna _____   I yma _____

GET FIT TIME! – HOW MANY REPS CAN YOU DO?

STRENGTH

Choose Your Exercise and Level
Watch exercise videos at www.summerfitlearning.com.

Leg Scissors   **Ankle Touches**   **Push-ups**

3-10 Reps   11-19 Reps   20-29 Reps

Measure using centimeters.

_____ centimeters

_____ centimeters   _____ centimeters

_____ centimeters

_____ centimeters   _____ centimeters

Need or want?

Needs are things we have to have to live a healthy life. Wants are things we would like but are not necessary.

Circle the needs, cross off the wants.

Week 6

67

Go to www.SummerFitLearning.com for Additional Games, Trivia and Activities!

GET FIT TIME – HOW LONG CAN YOU LAST?

AEROBIC

Choose Your Exercise and Level
Watch exercise videos at www.summerfitlearning.com.

Stepping Up	Hi-Yah	Swimming Scissors
10-30 Seconds	31-60 Seconds	61-90 Seconds

Write the number that comes before.

_____ 50   _____ 14   _____ 21   _____ 8

_____ 26   _____ 37   _____ 76   _____ 10

Write the number that comes between.

9 _____ 11   25 _____ 27   51 _____ 53

19 _____ 21   67 _____ 69   79 _____ 81

Finish the pattern:

1 _____ 6 _____ 12 _____ 18 _____ 24 _____ 30

Circle the largest number, cross off the smallest in each row.

55   67   75   63   36   66

42   38   44   89   98   88

Classifying. Cross out the object in each group that does not belong.

Go to www.SummerFitLearning.com for Additional Games, Trivia and Activities!

GET FIT TIME! – HOW MANY REPS CAN YOU DO?

STRENGTH

Choose Your Exercise and Level
Watch exercise videos at www.summerfitlearning.com.

Jumping Jacks	Jump Rope	Hula-hoop
3-10 Reps ☐	11-19 Reps ☐	20-29 Reps ☐

Draw the minute hand to show the time.

4:15   8:15   12:30   6:30

Write the temperatures.

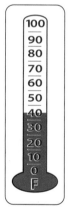
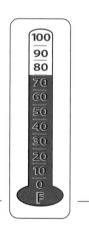
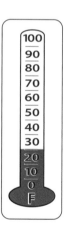

_____   _____

Color 1/6 of the crabs red.

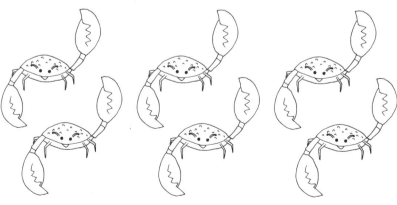

Go to www.SummerFitLearning.com for Additional Games, Trivia and Activities!

COURAGE

Courage means doing the right thing even when you are afraid, and you are the only one.

Rosa Parks

Rosa Parks was one of the heroes of the Civil Rights movement in the United States of America. Before the Civil Rights movement black people were not treated well. They had to sit in the back of busses and even had to give up their seat to white people. One day after work, Rosa got on the bus to go home. When the bus driver told Rosa to give up her seat for a white man she refused. Rosa showed courage by standing up for what was right even though she was afraid.

Circle the correct answer(s)

Rosa was asked to give up her _____.   purse   seat

Rosa was supposed to sit at the back of the bus because she was _____.   black   a woman

Rosa showed she had _____.   tired feet   courage

Rosa stood up for what was right for _____.   herself   everyone on the bus

GET FIT TIME – PLAY A SPORT

SPORT

Choose a Sport to Play

Use the sport index or www.summerfitlearning.com to choose a sport to play.

Try different sports. You can play with your family, friends, or by yourself. Have fun and play with good sportsmanship. Good sportsmanship means that you play fair and treat everyone with respect.

Booklist

Brave Irene
By William Steig

Cowardly Clyde
By Bill Peet

**Sheila Rae,
the Brave**
By Kevin Henkes

**Please visit
summerfitlearning.com
to download fun
summer book report
activity sheets.**

Courage Activities

Act out the story of Rosa Parks with your family or friends. Draw an outline of yourself on butcher paper. Write all the things about yourself that you are proud of. Write the words "The courage to be me" across the center. Hang it in your room.

Draw a picture or write a thank-you letter for a police officer or firefighter in your neighborhood. Thank them for the courage they show every day.

Let's Talk About It

Talk to your child about their fears. Help them find ways to face and overcome them. Share some of your fears when you were their age and how you faced them. Give them some examples of yourself and other family members having courage. Discuss people in your community who have shown great courage.

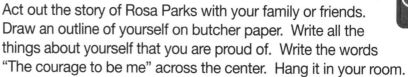

Go to www.SummerFitLearning.com for Additional Games, Trivia and Activities!

This Week We Will Cover

Abbreviations, community helpers, sounds of "sh" and "ch," asking and telling sentences, continents, fact families, addition and subtraction, map study, garden graph, tens and ones, counting backwards.

Don't Forget to Warm Up

Pick from the aerobic exercises, strength exercises and sport activities this week, but don't forget to warm up. It is always best to prepare your body for any physical activity by moving around and stretching first.

Walk or Jog: Walk or jog for 3-5 minutes to warm up before you exercise. Shake your arms and roll your shoulders when you are finished walking or jogging.

"V" Stretch: Sit on the ground with your legs out in front of you making a letter "V" shape. Reach for your toes again and count to 8 this time.

Neck stretch: While sitting or standing with your head in its normal upright position, slowly tilt it to the right until tension is felt on the left side of your neck. Hold that tension for 10 to 30 seconds and then return your head to the upright position.

Repeat to the left side, and then toward the front. Always return to the upright position before moving on.

Core Value For the Week RESPECT

Respect is honoring yourself and others. It is behaving in a way that makes life peaceful and orderly.

Sometimes we forget to appreciate that every person is unique and different, and that all of us want to be accepted and appreciated for who we are. Try to treat others the way that you want to be treated, even when it is difficult.

Respect in Action
I am showing respect when I...

Don't tease.

Take care of property.

Keep my hands to myself.

Obey the rules.

Am polite.

"If one doesn't respect oneself, one can have neither love nor respect for others."
– Ayn Rand

INCENTIVE CONTRACT

My incentive for completing this section will be:

_____

Signed (parent or guardian): _____

✓ off each day's exercises

	day 1	day 2	day 3	day 4	day 5
mind	☐	☐	☐	☐	☐
body	☐	☐	☐	☐	☐

values Write down three things you did this week to show your weekly value.

1. _____

2. _____

3. _____

CONGRATULATIONS

You did a terrific job this week!

Parent or Guardian signature: _____

Abbreviations are shortened words. Abbreviations usually begin with a capital and end with a period. Match each word with its abbreviation.

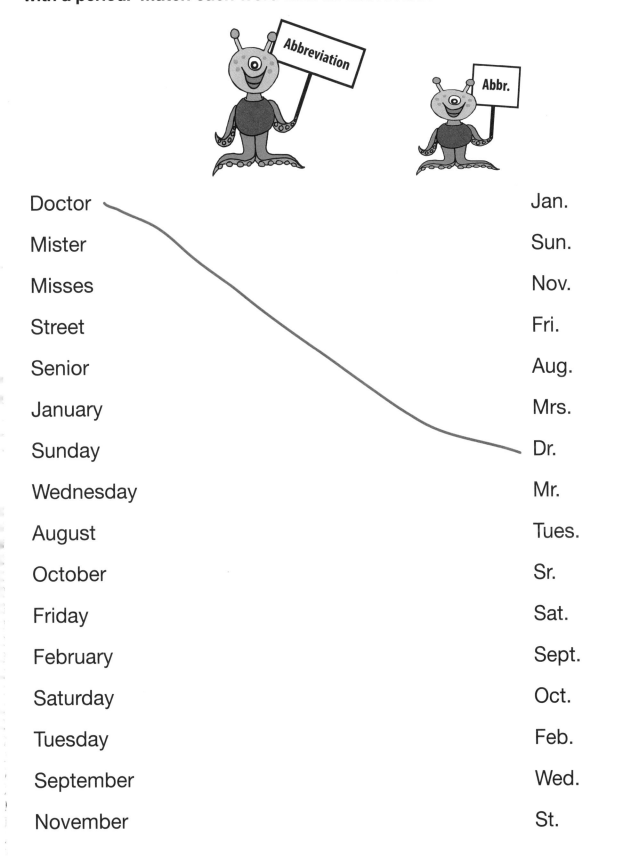

Doctor	Jan.
Mister	Sun.
Misses	Nov.
Street	Fri.
Senior	Aug.
January	Mrs.
Sunday	Dr.
Wednesday	Mr.
August	Tues.
October	Sr.
Friday	Sat.
February	Sept.
Saturday	Oct.
Tuesday	Feb.
September	Wed.
November	St.

GET FIT TIME – HOW LONG CAN YOU LAST?

AEROBIC

Choose Your Exercise and Level
Watch exercise videos at www.summerfitlearning.com.

Egg Race	Ball or Frisbee Toss and Run	Run or Jog
10-30 Seconds	31-60 Seconds	61-90 Seconds

Finish the fact family.

5 + 4 = 9

4 + 5 = 9

_____ - _____ = _____

_____ - _____ = _____

_____ + _____ = _____

_____ + _____ = _____

_____ - _____ = _____

_____ - _____ = _____

There were 8 frogs sitting on a log. 3 frogs jumped into the pond. How many frogs are left on the log? Why?

_____ frogs are left because _____ - _____ = _____

There are many people in our communities who help us. Solve the riddle by writing in the correct community helper on the line.

teacher	doctor	firefighter	police officer
dentist	mail carrier	bus driver	grocer

I deliver your mail and packages through rain or shine.   Who am I? _____

I make sure you stay healthy and help when you feel sick.   Who am I? _____

I keep the market stocked with healthy food for you to eat.   Who am I? _____

I work at school and help you learn to read, write and add.   Who am I? _____

I clean your teeth and make sure they stay healthy and strong.   Who am I? _____

I fight crime and help keep you safe in your community.   Who am I? _____

I help put out fires and rescue people who are in trouble.   Who am I? _____

GET FIT TIME! – HOW MANY REPS CAN YOU DO?

STRENGTH

Choose Your Exercise and Level
Watch exercise videos at www.summerfitlearning.com.

Fly in The Ointment	Jumping Jacks	Jump Rope
3-10 Reps ☐	11-19 Reps ☐	20-29 Reps ☐

North
West ←→ East
South

This is a map of Franklin Park.

If you walk from the trees to the play structure, which direction do you go?

_____

Where can you feed the ducks? _____

What is south of the dog park? _____

What is the name of this park? _____

To go from the pond to the dog park you would walk _____.

Fill in with "ch" or "sh" to complete each word.

_____ eep   _____ eese   _____ icken   _____ irt

_____ oe   fi _____   pea _____   _____ ip

Change the asking sentences into telling sentences.

Are we going to the beach?

_____

Did the chicken cross the road?

_____

Change the telling sentences into asking sentences.

The ship is sailing across the sea.

_____ ?

You can climb the peach tree.

_____ ?

Day 3

GET FIT TIME – HOW LONG CAN YOU LAST?

AEROBIC

Choose Your Exercise and Level
Watch exercise videos at www.summerfitlearning.com.

Freeze Tag   **Ghost Run or Jog**   **Dancing Shoes**

10-30 Seconds ☐   31-60 Seconds ☐   61-90 Seconds ■

Color one square for each item shown in the picture.

carrots										
cornstalks										
lettuce										
tomatoes										
squash										
pumpkins										

How many carrots and tomatoes altogether? _____ + _____ = _____

How many more heads of lettuce than squash? _____ - _____ = _____

How many corn and heads of lettuce together? _____ + _____ = _____

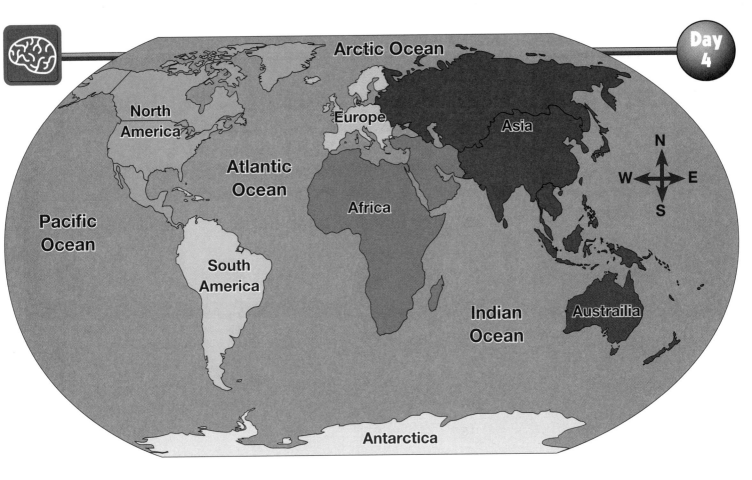

Look at the map and answer the questions.

A continent is a large body of land. Canada, Mexico and the United States are on North America. There are seven continents and four oceans on Earth.

Name the four oceans.

_____   _____

_____   _____

What continent is Canada and the United States on?_____

What is the biggest continent?_____

What continent is south of Asia?_____

What continent is west of Europe?_____

What continent is east of Africa?_____

GET FIT TIME! – HOW MANY REPS CAN YOU DO?

STRENGTH

Choose Your Exercise and Level
Watch exercise videos at www.summerfitlearning.com.

Jumping Jacks	Jump Rope	Hula-hoop
3-10 Reps	11-19 Reps	20-29 Reps

Circle the sum or difference.

10 – 5 =   four   five   six

8 + 2 =   ten   nine   eight

10 - 3 =   six   seven   eight

3 + 3 =   nine   six   four

Draw a circle around ten of the stars. Write the number of tens and ones.

tens	ones

tens	ones

tens	ones

tens	ones

Count backwards by 10s.

100 _____ _____ _____ 60 _____ _____ _____ 20 _____

 **RESPECT**

Respect is being nice to yourself and others.

Mohandas Gandhi

Mohandas Gandhi was born on October 2, 1869. He was a gentle boy while growing up and became a strong and respected leader in India. Gandhi taught that if you hurt someone else you are also hurting yourself. He showed people how to accept each other even if they were different. He believed there would be peace in the world if everyone would respect and accept each other.

Fill in the blanks to complete the sentences.

Mohandas Ghandi was known as the Father of I ___ ___ ___ ___.

He believed in peace not w___ ____.

Ghandi wanted all people to r___ ___ ___ ___ ___ ___ each other.

Week 7

83

Go to www.SummerFitLearning.com for Additional Games, Trivia and Activities!

GET FIT TIME – PLAY A SPORT

SPORT

Choose a Sport to Play

Use the sport index or www.summerfitlearning.com to choose a sport to play.

Try different sports. You can play with your family, friends, or by yourself. Have fun and play with good sportsmanship. Good sportsmanship means that you play fair and treat everyone with respect.

Booklist

All the Colors of the Earth
By Sheila Hamanaka

The Berenstain Bears Forget Their Manners
By Stan and Jan Berenstain

Leo the Late Bloomer
By Robert Kraus

Please visit summerfitlearning.com to download fun summer book report activity sheets.

Respect Activities

Visit the library and learn about the rules the library uses while you are there. Why is it important to respect property? How do you take care of things you borrow?

Write out the Golden Rule: "Do unto others as you would have them do unto you." Decorate it and hang it up in a place where you will see it and be reminded to live it.

Make up a song, chant, or rap about respect. Tell why respect is important and how it can make the world a better place. Teach it to your friends and family.

Let's Talk About It

Talk to your kids about how important respect is and why. Discuss what it means to respect themselves, others, property, space, beliefs, etc. Make sure they understand that they must respect themselves first, before they will be able to respect others. Help them come up with ways to show respect in their everyday life.

This Week We Will Cover

Homophones, your family tree, pronouns, healthy food choices, hundreds chart, follow directions, finish the pattern, 10 less, counting coins, estimation, time.

Don't Forget to Warm Up

Pick from the aerobic exercises, strength exercises and sport activities this week but don't forget to warm up. It is always best to prepare your body for any physical activity by moving around and stretching first.

Walk or Jog: Walk or jog for 3-5 minutes to warm up before you exercise. Shake your arms and roll your shoulders when you are finished walking or jogging.

Reach to the sky: Stand with feet shoulder-width apart. Raise both arms overhead so that your hands are intertwined with palms together. Hold for 10 to 30 seconds and relax.

Chest Stretch: In a standing position lift your arms overhead. Bend your elbows and clasp your fingers behind your head. Draw your elbows back as you press your chest forward. Hold for 30 seconds.

Core Value For the Week
RESPONSIBILITY

Being responsible means others can depend on you. It is being accountable for what you do and for what you do not do.

A lot of times it is easier to look to someone else to step forward and do the work or to blame when it does not get done. You are smart, capable and able, so try to be the person who accepts challenges and does not blame others if it does not get done.

Responsibility in Action
I am responsible when I...

Keep my promises.

Follow the rules.

Do my best in everything.

Admit my mistakes.

"The ability to accept responsibility is the measure of a man."
- Roy L. Smith

INCENTIVE CONTRACT

My incentive for completing this section will be:

_____

Signed (parent or guardian): _____

✓ off each day's exercises

	day 1	day 2	day 3	day 4	day 5
mind	☐	☐	☐	☐	☐
body	☐	☐	☐	☐	☐

values Write down three things you did this week to show your weekly value.

1. _____

2. _____

3. _____

CONGRATULATIONS

You did a terrific job this week!

Parent or Guardian signature: _____

Words that sound the same but are spelled differently and have different meanings are called homophones.

Color each set of fish with sound-alike words the same color.

Go to www.SummerFitLearning.com for Additional Games, Trivia and Activities!

GET FIT TIME – HOW LONG CAN YOU LAST?

AEROBIC

Choose Your Exercise and Level
Watch exercise videos at www.summerfitlearning.com.

Wheel Over	Hide and Seek	Jumping Jacks
10-30 Seconds	31-60 Seconds	61-90 Seconds ▮

Odd or even?

1	2	3	4	5	6	7	8	9	10
11	12	13	14	15	16	17	18	19	20
21	22	23	24	25	26	27	28	29	30
31	32	33	34	35	36	37	38	39	40
41	42	43	44	45	46	47	48	49	50
51	52	53	54	55	56	57	58	59	60
61	62	63	64	65	66	67	68	69	70
71	72	73	74	75	76	77	78	79	80
81	82	83	84	85	86	87	88	89	90
91	92	93	94	95	96	97	98	99	100

Starting with 1, color every other number green. Color the rest of the numbers blue. Follow this pattern: 1 = green, 2= blue, 3 = green, 4 = blue, etc.
The blue numbers are even, which means they can be split evenly into two numbers.
The green numbers are odd, which means they cannot be divided evenly into two numbers.

Write 3 **even** numbers_____

Write 3 **odd** numbers_____

Go to www.SummerFitLearning.com for Additional Games, Trivia and Activities!

My family tree.

With you parent's help fill in this family tree. Add the names of your parents, siblings and grandparents.

_____
_____

_____   _____   _____
_____   _____   _____
_____   _____   _____
_____   _____

Grandparents   _____   **Grandparents**

Siblings

_____

Me

_____   _____
Father   **Mother**

Week 8   89

Go to www.SummerFitLearning.com for Additional Games, Trivia and Activities!

GET FIT TIME! – HOW MANY REPS CAN YOU DO?

STRENGTH

Choose Your Exercise and Level
Watch exercise videos at www.summerfitlearning.com.

Ankle Touches   **Push-ups**   **Moon Touches**

3-10 Reps   11-19 Reps   20-29 Reps

My important numbers. Fill in the numbers that help tell about you. Ask your parents if you need some help.

My birth date_____

My phone number _____

My street address _____

My parents cell-phone number _____

I am _____ years old.

My name has _____ letters in it.

I have _____ people in my family.

Finish the pattern.

A, B, A, B, _____,_____, _____, _____, _____, _____, _____, _____, _____, _____, _____, _____

1, 2, 3, 1, 2, 3, _____,_____, _____, _____, _____, _____, _____, _____, _____, _____, _____, _____

Pronouns are words that can take the place of nouns.

Use a pronoun to complete each sentence.

he	she	it	they
her	them	him	we

Mom likes to bake. _____ makes tasty cookies.

Gabe and John like to play ball. _____ are on the soccer team.

Grace and I are going to the park. _____ will go on the swings.

The balloon got stuck in the tree. _____ popped.

Noah got some cars for his birthday. _____ played with _____ all day.

Jane was late and missed _____ bus.

I am going to visit my grandparents. I will stay with _____ for a week.

GET FIT TIME – HOW LONG CAN YOU LAST?

AEROBIC

Choose Your Exercise and Level

Watch exercise videos at www.summerfitlearning.com.

Turtle and Rabbit

Cross Country Skier

Tree Sprints

10-30 Seconds ☐   31-60 Seconds ☐   61-90 Seconds ☐

Draw a line from each alien to the spaceship that is 10 less.

Ex:

11   12   15   16   18   19   17   14   13

1   2   3   4   5   6   7   8   9

Circle the bank with the most money.

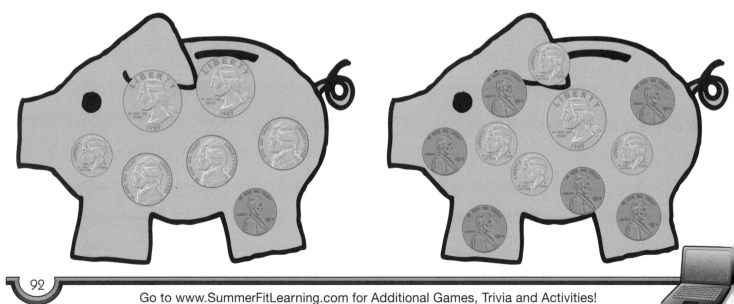

Go to www.SummerFitLearning.com for Additional Games, Trivia and Activities!

Eating healthy food will make me strong.

Foods that are good for me can be divided into 4 groups: breads and grains, meats and protein, vegetables and fruits, and milk and cheese (dairy).

Circle the healthy foods. Cross off the foods that are not healthy.

Draw a picture of a healthy dinner.
Choose 1 item from each of the 4 groups.

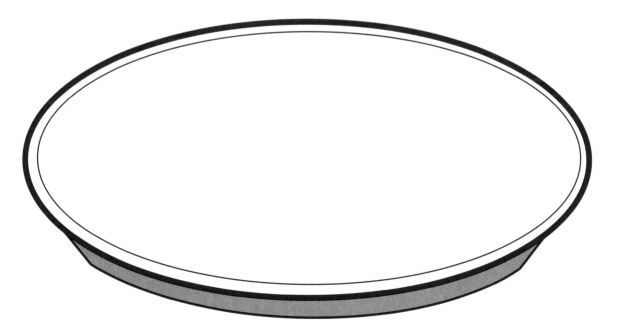

Go to www.SummerFitLearning.com for Additional Games, Trivia and Activities!

GET FIT TIME! – HOW MANY REPS CAN YOU DO?

STRENGTH

Choose Your Exercise and Level
Watch exercise videos at www.summerfitlearning.com.

Push-ups   **Moon Touches**   **Chop and Squat**

3-10 Reps   11-19 Reps   20-29 Reps

To estimate is to make a guess about something using the information you know. Circle the best estimate.

95 cents   10 cents $100.00

$95.00 $10.00 $1.00

15 cents   80 cents $15.00

$15.00 $8.00 $15,000.00

Look at the clock. What time will it be in 1 hour?

_____ : _____

Go to www.SummerFitLearning.com for Additional Games, Trivia and Activities!

RESPONSIBILITY

Responsibility includes doing the things you know that you should, and doing something with the challenges in life you don't expect.

Terrance Stanley Fox was a very good athlete. His favorite sport was basketball but he also played rugby, golf and ran cross country in high school. Sadly, Terry lost one of his legs because he got cancer, and he felt it was his responsibility to do all that he could for other people with cancer. Even though it was very hard, he set off to run across Canada with an artificial leg to raise money for cancer research. He called his run the Marathon of Hope. When he started to run not many people knew about Terry or what he was doing but now people all over the world participate or take part in an event named after Terry to raise money for cancer research.

© Photo courtesy of the Terry Fox Foundation

www.terryfox.org

Draw a picture of yourself being responsible.

Week 8

Go to www.SummerFitLearning.com for Additional Games, Trivia and Activities!

95

Day 5

GET FIT TIME – PLAY A SPORT

SPORT

Choose a Sport to Play

Use the sport index or www.summerfitlearning.com to choose a sport to play.

Try different sports. You can play with your family, friends, or by yourself. Have fun and play with good sportsmanship. Good sportsmanship means that you play fair and treat everyone with respect.

Booklist

Horton Hatches the Egg
By Dr. Seuss

Pigsty
By Mark Teague

Arthur's Computer Disaster
By Marc Brown

Please visit summerfitlearning.com to download fun summer book report activity sheets.

Responsibility Activities

Be responsible for the earth. Make a list of things your family can do to save water, recycle and help clean up your neighborhood.

Plan and practice a fire drill in your home. Write down your plan and make sure every member of the family knows what their responsibility is.

If you are responsible for a pet, draw a poster showing all the things you need to do to take care of it.

Let's Talk About It

Discuss and role-play the many opportunities to be responsible at home and at school. Talk about what it means to be accountable for what you say and do. Make sure your child understands that part of learning to be responsible is admitting when you make a mistake.

Stepping Stones

Stepping Stones Entertainment™ was founded by parents who wanted to provide meaningful family movies to help inspire common values. It is made up of people from many different backgrounds, nationalities and beliefs. For more than 20 years, Stepping Stones has provided families with movies about integrity, charity, forgiveness and many other common values through hundreds of films for all ages. Learn more at **www.steppingstones.com**.

STEPPING STONES.COM
Meaningful Family Movies

96

Go to www.SummerFitLearning.com for Additional Games, Trivia and Activities!

This Week We Will Cover

USA symbols, following directions, adjectives, finish the sentence, units of measurement, sums, divide by 2, even and odd numbers, time, count by 10s, tally marks, <,>,or =.

Don't Forget to Warm Up

Pick from the aerobic exercises, strength exercises and sport activities this week, but don't forget to warm up. It is always best to prepare your body for any physical activity by moving around and stretching first.

Walk or Jog: Walk or jog for 3-5 minutes to warm up before you exercise. Shake your arms and roll your shoulders when you are finished walking or jogging.

Wall Stretch: Stand facing a wall. Place your right palm on the wall so it's in line with your shoulder, and point your fingers back. Keep your right hand planted firmly, and bend your left arm behind you. Now walk a few small steps to the left and stop when you feel a good stretch in your right shoulder and chest. Hold for 30 seconds and then walk back towards the wall.

"I am a slow walker but I never walk backwards" - Abraham Lincoln

"V" Stretch: Sit on the ground with your legs out in front of you making a letter "V" shape. Reach for your toes again and count to 8 this time.

Core Value For the Week
PERSEVERENCE

Perseverance means not giving up or giving in when things are difficult. It means you try again when you fail.

Sometimes it is easy to forget that a lot of things in life require patience and hard work. Do not give up because it is hard to accomplish a task or to get something that we want. Focus on your goal and keep working hard. It is through this experience that you will accomplish what you set out to do.

Perseverence in Action
I am showing perseverance when I...

When I make a mistake, try again.

Am patient with myself and others.

Finish what I start.

Don't give up.

INCENTIVE CONTRACT

My incentive for completing this section will be:

_____

Signed (parent or guardian): _____

✔ off each day's exercises

	day 1	day 2	day 3	day 4	day 5
mind	☐	☐	☐	☐	☐
body	☐	☐	☐	☐	☐

values

Write down three things you did this week to show your weekly value.

1. _____

2. _____

3. _____

CONGRATULATIONS

You did a terrific job this week!

Parent or Guardian signature: _____

There are many symbols that remind us of the United States of America. Using the words below, complete each sentence.

bald eagle   Statue of Liberty   Canada "Star Spangled Banner"   Liberty Bell   American flag U. S. Capitol   Mexico

The _____ has 50 stars and 13 red and white stripes.

The _____ is a symbol of America's freedom from Britain.

The _____ was a gift from France and stands for freedom.

_____ is the USA neighbor to the south.

This is the _____. It is in Washington, D.C.

The _____is the USA's national anthem and was written by Francis Scott Key.

The _____ is the USA's national bird and stands for strength and courage.

_____ is the USA neighbor to the north.

Week 9

99

Go to www.SummerFitLearning.com for Additional Games, Trivia and Activities!

GET FIT TIME – HOW LONG CAN YOU LAST?

AEROBIC

Choose Your Exercise and Level
Watch exercise videos at www.summerfitlearning.com.

Foot Bag	Tag	Wheel Over
10-30 Seconds	31-60 Seconds	61-90 Seconds

Draw a line to match the measurements.

1 hour	16 ounces
1 yard	12 months
1 minute	60 minutes
1 year	3 feet
1 pound	60 seconds

Write the sums to complete the equations.

6 + 2 + 3 = _____   7 + 1 + 3 = _____   8 + 2 + 4 = _____

How many cents do these coins total?

=_____cents

=_____cents

Go to www.SummerFitLearning.com for Additional Games, Trivia and Activities!

Following directions.

Write numbers 1–5 to put the directions in the right order.

_____Get your toothbrush and toothpaste.

_____Put everything away.

_____Rinse your toothbrush.

_____Put toothpaste on your toothbrush.

_____Brush your teeth.

_____Put on a stamp.

_____Mail the letter.

_____Address the envelope.

_____Write the letter and seal it in the envelope.

_____Get paper, envelope and a stamp.

Week 9

101

Go to www.SummerFitLearning.com for Additional Games, Trivia and Activities!

GET FIT TIME! – HOW MANY REPS CAN YOU DO?

STRENGTH

Choose Your Exercise and Level
Watch exercise videos at www.summerfitlearning.com.

Fly in The Ointment

3-10 Reps

Jumping Jacks

11-19 Reps

Jump Rope

20-29 Reps

Write 1/2 of each number.

½ of 10 = _____

½ of 12 = _____

½ of 14 = _____

½ of 16 = _____

½ of 18 = _____

½ of 20 = _____

Color the even numbers purple and the odd numbers yellow.

Write + or – to get the correct answer.

6 _____ 4 = 10

10 _____ 5 = 5

8 _____ 3 = 11

12 _____ 6 = 6

Go to www.SummerFitLearning.com for Additional Games, Trivia and Activities!

Adjectives are words that describe something. Circle the adjective in each phrase, then draw a line to the picture that matches.

Blue bird

Stinky sock

Slimy worm

Hot day

Soft cat

Rainy day

Spotted dog

Go to www.SummerFitLearning.com for Additional Games, Trivia and Activities!

GET FIT TIME - HOW LONG CAN YOU LAST?

AEROBIC

Choose Your Exercise and Level
Watch exercise videos at www.summerfitlearning.com.

Ball or Frisbee Toss and Run	Turtle and Rabbit	Jumping Jacks
10-30 Seconds □	31-60 Seconds □	61-90 Seconds ■

What time is it?

_____   _____   _____

Circle 1 dozen bagels.

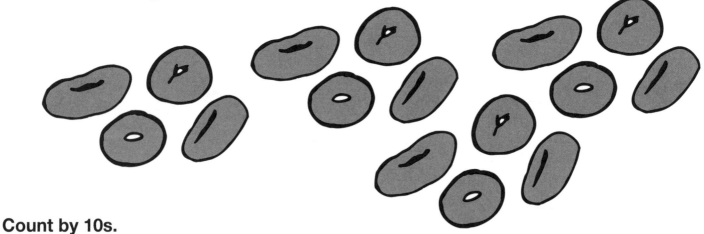

Count by 10s.

120 _____ 140 _____ 160 _____ 180 _____ 200

Day 4

Pick a word to finish each sentence.

The dog dug a hole for his _____.

The girl dressed her _____ for the party.

Sam read 10 pages of his _____ after dinner.

John David wore his _____ to go sledding.

The farmer grew a crop of _____.

The _____ are growing in the garden.

Week 9

105

Go to www.SummerFitLearning.com for Additional Games, Trivia and Activities!

GET FIT TIME! – HOW MANY REPS CAN YOU DO?

STRENGTH

Choose Your Exercise and Level
Watch exercise videos at www.summerfitlearning.com.

Moon Touches	Chop and Squat	Fly in The Ointment
3-10 Reps ☐	11-19 Reps ☐	20-29 Reps ☐

Write <, >, or = to show which number is higher and lower. The arrow always points to the smaller number.

1/2 _____ 1/4   100 _____ 110

3 + 3 _____ 4 + 2   24 _____ 42

5 – 3 _____ 6 - 2   1/2 _____ 2/4

Draw tally marks for each number.

5   12   9   16

_____   _____   _____   _____

There were 9 girls and 8 boys swimming at the pool. How many children were swimming at the pool?

_____ + _____ = _____

Go to www.SummerFitLearning.com for Additional Games, Trivia and Activities!

Perseverance is the act of not giving up and not giving in.

Spoungeworthy Photo by Phil Stefans

Bethany Hamilton

Bethany Hamilton was sitting on her surfboard one sunny day in Hawaii, waiting for the next big wave. Suddenly a shark attacked her and she was left without her arm. Thirteen-year old Bethany survived and was soon surfing again. Getting back in the water meant overcoming her fear of another attack and learning to surf again with only one arm. Bethany kept at it and persevered by never giving up on her dreams even when they seemed impossible.

Fill in the blanks using the words from the box.

surf   dreams   shark   fear   arm

Bethany was attacked by a _____. She lost her _____.

Bethany overcame her _____.

She learned to _____ again.

Bethany never gave up on her _____.

Week 9   107

Go to www.SummerFitLearning.com for Additional Games, Trivia and Activities!

GET FIT TIME – PLAY A SPORT

SPORT

Choose a Sport to Play

Use the sport index or www.summerfitlearning.com to choose a sport to play.

Try different sports. You can play with your family, friends, or by yourself. Have fun and play with good sportsmanship. Good sportsmanship means that you play fair and treat everyone with respect.

Booklist

D. W. Flips
By Marc Brown

Pancakes for Breakfast
By Tommie DePaola

Katie and the Big Snow
By Virginia L. Burton

Please visit summerfitlearning.com to download fun summer book report activity sheets.

Perseverance Activities

Try learning a new sport or game. Keep practicing and don't give up.

Decorate a clay pot, fill it with soil and plant flower seeds. As you watch the flower grow, remember that the plant is like perseverance, starting off small and growing little by little.

Spiders show perseverance when they build their webs. Some spiders have to rebuild their web each day. Look for books on spiders and learn about how a web is made. Make a picture of a spider and its web.

Let's Talk About It

Perseverance helps our children be successful and boosts their self-esteem. Help them set goals for themselves and to be self-motivated. Encourage them in the things they struggle with but let them know it is okay. They don't always have to be the best at everything, but they do have to try their best at everything they do.

108

Go to www.SummerFitLearning.com for Additional Games, Trivia and Activities!

This Week We Will Cover

Missing letters "oa" and "ou", sight words, word scramble, beavers, creative writing, counting coins, fill in the missing numbers, <,>,=, fractions, write before and after numbers by 5, subtraction of 2 digit numbers, least to greatest, tally marks, and finish the pattern.

Don't Forget to Warm Up

Pick from the aerobic exercises, strength exercises and sport activities this week but don't forget to warm up. It is always best to prepare your body for any physical activity by moving around and stretching first.

Walk or Jog: Walk or jog for 3-5 minutes to warm up before you exercise. Shake your arms and roll your shoulders when you are finished walking or jogging.

Standing Side Stretch: Stretch your right arm all the way up and over to your left side. Curve your body while you do this, so you'll be looking sideways. Hold it by counting all the way to 10. Then d o the same thing with the left arm. Remember to count all the way to 10 before you let go.

Sky Stretch: Reach both hands up very- very high! Try to reach so high that you touch the sky! Next, reach all the way down, down, down all the way to your toes. Try to keep your legs straight when you touch your toes. Let's hold this for 10 counts.

Core Value For the Week
Friendship

Friendship is what comes from being friends. It is caring and sharing and being there for each other in good times and bad.

It is fun to have friends that we play with, go to the movies and share our time, but it also is a responsibility. Our friends are people that we trust, protect, respect and stand up for even when it is not easy. We care about our friends and our friends care about us.

Friendship in Action
I am practicing friendship when I...

Am dependable.

Am a good listener.

Am a friend in good times and bad.

Am loyal.

Keep promises.

"Little friends may prove great friends"
- Aesop

INCENTIVE CONTRACT

My incentive for completing this section will be:

_____

Signed (parent or guardian): _____

✔ off each day's exercises

	day 1	day 2	day 3	day 4	day 5
mind	☐	☐	☐	☐	☐
body	☐	☐	☐	☐	☐

values

Write down three things you did this week to show your weekly value.

1. _____

2. _____

3. _____

CONGRATULATIONS

You did a terrific job this week!

Parent or Guardian signature: _____

Fill in the missing letters "oa" or "ou" to complete each word.

b____t   h____se   c____t

s____p   h____nd   t____d

m____se   r____d   g____t

Read these sight words to an adult.

In	And	Are
We	The	Them
Out	Do	Some
Could	shall	by
Look	was	have
They	were	you
With	want	of

Week 10

Go to www.SummerFitLearning.com for Additional Games, Trivia and Activities!

111

GET FIT TIME – HOW LONG CAN YOU LAST?

AEROBIC

Choose Your Exercise and Level
Watch exercise videos at www.summerfitlearning.com.

Run or Jog	Egg Race	Jumping Jacks
10-30 Seconds	31-60 Seconds	61-90 Seconds

Match the coins with object they will buy.

75¢

95¢

65¢

49¢

Fill in the missing numbers.

2 ____ 6 ____ 10 ____ 14 ____ 18 ____ 22 ____ 26 ____ 30

5, 10 ____ 20 ____ 30 ____ 40 ____ 50 ____ 60 ____ 70 ____

Go to www.SummerFitLearning.com for Additional Games, Trivia and Activities!

At the beach.

Unscramble the mixed up letters to make words of what you might see at the beach. Then draw a line from the word to its picture.

liap   _____

snusglases   _____

labl   _____

murbllea   _____

evwas   _____

snda cstela   _____

trassfih   _____

hsvole   _____

Week 10

Go to www.SummerFitLearning.com for Additional Games, Trivia and Activities!

113

GET FIT TIME! – HOW MANY REPS CAN YOU DO?

STRENGTH

Choose Your Exercise and Level
Watch exercise videos at www.summerfitlearning.com.

Moon Touches

3-10 Reps

Chop and Squat

11-19 Reps

Fly in The Ointment

20-29 Reps

Color 1 equal part. Circle the name of the part you colored.

1/4   1/3   1/2

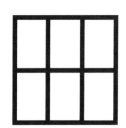

1/4   1/5   1/6

1/3   1/2   1/4

Write the before and after numbers by 5s.

_____25_____ , _____15_____ , _____60_____

Write the differences to solve the equations.

50 – 30 = _____   90 – 50 = _____

30 – 10 = _____   100 – 50 = _____

80 – 70 = _____   60 – 40 = _____

20 – 20 = _____   70 – 30 = _____

Busy as a Beaver

Beavers are interesting animals. They are dark brown and usually weigh between 30 and 60 pounds. The beaver's tail is very thick and is shaped like a large paddle at the end. Beavers have huge front teeth and only eat plants, bark from trees, and twigs. Beavers are excellent swimmers and live in streams and lakes with trees nearby. They spend their time cutting tree limbs and branches with their teeth. They drag branches to the site of their lodge, where they make a stick and mud dam. Beavers have only one mate, and live together in families.

Circle the correct answer.

Beavers are.	brown	black
Beavers eat.	plants and trees	meat
A beaver's house is called a.	condo	lodge
A beaver has a thick tail shaped like a.	baseball	paddle
Beaver's live.	in the ocean	in lakes and streams
Beavers use sticks and branches to build a.	dam	cabin

GET FIT TIME - HOW LONG CAN YOU LAST?

AEROBIC

Choose Your Exercise and Level
Watch exercise videos at www.summerfitlearning.com.

Ball or Frisbee Toss and Run   **Hi-Yah**   **Tree Sprints**

10-30 Seconds   31-60 Seconds   61-90 Seconds

Circle the correct answer.

An hour is _____ minutes.

60   45

A day is _____ hours.

30   24

A year is _____ months.

12   10

A dozen is _____ .

2   12

Write the numbers from least to greatest.

180   108   80   188   118

_____   _____   _____   _____   _____

Complete the pattern.

10, 12, 14, _____, _____, _____

3, 6, 9, _____, _____, _____

Go to www.SummerFitLearning.com for Additional Games, Trivia and Activities!

Write a story telling what is in the sack.

Use colorful words to describe (adjectives) and interesting action words (verbs). Read it to your family when you are done.

_____

_____

_____

_____

_____

_____

_____

_____

_____

_____

_____

_____

Week 10

117

Go to www.SummerFitLearning.com for Additional Games, Trivia and Activities!

Day
4

GET FIT TIME! – HOW MANY REPS CAN YOU DO?

STRENGTH

Choose Your Exercise and Level
Watch exercise videos at www.summerfitlearning.com.

Leg Scissors	Ankle Touches	Push-ups
3-10 Reps ▢	11-19 Reps ▢	20-29 Reps ▢

Draw 2 flowers in each vase.

There are _____ vases.   _____ flowers in each vase.   _____ flowers in all.

Color the digit in the tens place.

Color the digit in the ones place.

118

Go to www.SummerFitLearning.com for Additional Games, Trivia and Activities!

Friendship is what comes from being friends. It is caring and being there for each other.

Lewis and Clark

Meriwether Lewis and William Clark were friends over 200 years ago when the United States of America was still a new country. Together they went on an adventure that took them from the Mississippi River west to the Pacific Ocean. U.S. President Thomas Jefferson wanted them to explore the land, begin trading with Native-American tribes, find new plants and animals, and make maps of their journey. The journey took over two years and was very dangerous. Through it all Lewis and Clark stood by each other and supported each other with kindness, bravery, and loyalty. Lewis and Clark became two of America's greatest explorers.

Lewis and Clark kept notebooks and journals of all the new plants and animals they discovered. Draw a line from each picture to its name.

Bighorn sheep

Prickly pear

Porcupine

California condor

North American Badger

Week 10

Go to www.SummerFitLearning.com for Additional Games, Trivia and Activities!

119

GET FIT TIME – PLAY A SPORT

SPORT

Choose a Sport to Play

Use the sport index or www.summerfitlearning.com to choose a sport to play.

Try different sports. You can play with your family, friends, or by yourself. Have fun and play with good sportsmanship. Good sportsmanship means that you play fair and treat everyone with respect.

Booklist

We Are Best Friends
By Aliki

Stellaluna
By Jannell Cannon

Koko's Kitten
By Dr. Francine Patterson

Please visit summerfitlearning.com to download fun summer book report activity sheets.

Friendship Activities

Invite your friends over to make a "Friendship Fruit Salad." Ask everyone to bring their favorite fruit cut up… apples, bananas, pineapple, strawberries, etc. Combine them in a bowl and talk about all the ingredients needed for a good friendship.

Draw a picture for one of your friends. Roll it up, tie it with ribbon and deliver it.

Find a photo of you and a friend or have your parents take one. Make a frame using Popsicle sticks, twigs, shells or whatever else you can think of.

Let's Talk About It

Discuss true friendship with your child. Role-play different ways to make and keep friends. Teach them the quote "The only way to have a friend is to be a friend." Talk about what that means.

Stepping Stones

Stepping Stones Entertainment™ was founded by parents who wanted to provide meaningful family movies to help inspire common values. It is made up of people from many different backgrounds, nationalities and beliefs. For more than 20 years, Stepping Stones has provided families with movies about integrity, charity, forgiveness and many other common values through hundreds of films for all ages. Learn more at **www.steppingstones.com**.

Go to www.SummerFitLearning.com for Additional Games, Trivia and Activities!

Way to GO! You are finished!

Use this Answer Section
on the following pages to check your work.
While you're at it, check out your new muscles!

YOUR BRAIN AND BODY THANK YOU FOR ALL YOUR HARD WORK!

Week 1 Day 1
do(g), brea(d), su(n), ra(m), sta(r), ha(t), to(p)
a, u, i, e, o

Add or subtract:
2, 8, 1, 3
6, 3, 8, 10
Circle the right amount of coins:
1 quarter, 1 nickel, 2 dimes
1 nickel, 2 dimes
Count by 2s:
4, 8, 12, 16, 20

Week 1 Day 2
Circle the healthy choices:
bike
boy with ball
boy walking dog
apple
toothbrush
boy with swimsuit

How many inches:
worm = 4 inches
grasshopper = 2 inches
fly = 1 inch
feather = 5 inches
comb = 3 inches

Week 1 Day 3
Short or long:
short, long
Short vowel sounds:
pin, top, cat, cup
Long vowel sounds:
kite, feet, mule, ape, rope

Look at the time:
on time. early. late
Count by 5s:
10, 20, 30, 40, 50, 60, 70, 80, 90, 100

Week 1 Day 4
Let's go to the zoo:
Yes, Yes
zookeepers
A zoo is a place to see animals.
Circle the nouns in each house:
cat, moon, book, dog
cup, bug, ape, bat
nest, sun, egg, bee
man, zoo, car, tree
gate, lake, fish

Week 1 Day 5:
tell her what happened
turn it in to the librarian
clean your room

Week 2 Day 1
More than, less than:
3 < 9   7 > 5
11 > 10 0 < 1
15 < 20 10 > 3
Finish the pattern:
circle, circle, square, triangle
Circle each honest choice:
tell her what happened.
turn it in to the librarian.
clean your room.
Count by 3s:
6, 12, 18, 24, 30
How many cents:
82 cents

Week 2 Day 2
Doubles:
$3 + 3 = 6$ $4 + 4 = 8$
$6 + 6 = 12$ $1 + 1 = 2$ $5 + 5 = 10$

Week 2 Day 3
Draw a line to match the words to the contractions:
do not = don't
cannot = can't
she is = she's
it is = it's
he is = he's
we are = we're
they will = they'll
I have = I've
will not = won't

Adding and subtracting 10s:
4 tens, 2 tens, 5 tens, 3 tens
Solve each problem:
30 cents, 20 bugs

Week 2 Day 4
a, u, i, o, e
u, i, a, e, o
Write the days of the week:
Sunday =   Sun.
Monday =   Mon.
Tuesday =   Tues.
Wednesday =   Wed.
Thursday =   Thurs.
Friday =   Fri.

Write the time:
5:00, 3:00, 12:30, 6:00
9:30, 4:00, 2:30, 10:00
Use these words to fill in the blank:
compassion
poor
others
cared

Week 3 Day 1
Circle the verbs:
run, see, play, swim, sleep, smell, fly
Use the verbs above to finish the sentences:
play, smell, sleep, fly, hide

Write the number that is one more:
26, 14, 37, 10
Write >, <, or =:
<, >, <
=, >, =

Week 3 Day 2
Write the words in alphabetical order:
at   man
bat   pan
cat   ran
fan   rat
fat   tan

Circle the shape that matches the word:
red oval
green triangle
purple rectangle
blue square
10 cents, 40 cents, 70 cents
20 cents, 50 cents, 80 cents
30 cents, 60 cents, 90 cents

Week 3 Day 3
Calendar Days:
January
February
December
30 days
[child's birthday month]
Synonyms:
Happy – Glad
Small – Tiny
Large – Big
Begin – Start
Cold – Chilly
Mad – Angry
Ill – Sick

Week 3 Day 4
Number the parts of the stories in the correct order:
4, 1, 3, 2
4, 1, 3, 2
Count by 5s to 100:
15, 20, 25,
30, 35, 40, 45, 50,
55, 60, 65, 70, 75,
80, 85, 90, 95, 100
Add:
6, 8, 8, 9, 8

Answers

Week 3 Day 5
Draw a picture of you being trustworthy

Week 4 Day 1
Write the singular form:

car	ball
box	truck
shirt	fox
girl	dress

Write the new word:
babies
bunnies
stories
guppies

Find the total value:
1 ten 2 ones = 12
1 ten 3 ones = 13
1 ten 4 ones = 14
1 ten 5 ones = 15
2 tens 0 ones = 20
2 tens 1 ones = 21
3 tens 2 ones = 32
4 tens 3 ones = 43
4 tens 4 ones = 44

Week 4 Day 2
The dog is playing with a ball.
It is warm today.
I am riding the bike.
Add the correct punctuation:
?

.

?

.

Circle the larger number:
28, 13, 51
31, 10, 32
45, 20, 15
Finish the pattern:
10, 20, 30, 40, 50, 60

Week 4 Day 3
Circle the adjectives:
Red
Blue
Slimy
Fast
Soft
Tiny
Hot
[fill in your own adjectives]

Count how many of each pet:
Dogs
5 more
Fish
Grasshopper

Week 4 Day 4
Compound words:
Birdhouse
Snowman
Football
Haystack
Fireman
Airplane
Cupcake

Fact families:
7, 7, 8, 8
3, 4, 6, 2
8, 6
4, 10
12, 14

Week 4 Day 5
Stephanie helps kids in foster care
Draw a picture of her helping kids

Week 5 Day 1
[label the parts of the ant]
Circle the correct answer:
queen
strong
antennae
6

Fill in the numbers from 51 to 100:
52, 54, 56, 58, 60
62, 64, 66, 68, 70
72, 74, 76, 78, 80
82, 84, 86, 88, 90
92, 94, 96, 98, 100
Circle the unit of measurement:
inches
yards
pounds
ounces
quarts
gallons

Week 5 Day 2
I see the cat on the mat.
The man had a bag of sand.
I can swim all day.
[circle each "!"]

How many sides and corners?
4 sides, 4 corners 8 sides, 8 corners
3 sides, 4 corners 5 sides, 5 corners
Label each part:

½	1/3
¼	¼
½	½

2, 3
4

Week 5 Day 3
up – down
strong – weak
fast – slow
over – under
in – out
clean – dirty
tall – short

[color the shapes]
Mark >, <, or =:
<, =, >
>, >, =
<, <, >
>, <, <
>, <, >
<, >, >

Week 5 Day 4
Fill in missing letters:
oa, ee, oa, ee, oa
oa, ee, oa, oa, ee
Add an "e" at end of each word:

bite	kite
cane	mane
vane	cape
tape	mate

Problems to solve:
32 – 10 = 22
15 + 13 = 28
60 – 30 = 30
16, 24
35, 68
59, 64

Week 5 Day 5
Do what is written on the hearts to
show kindness

Week 6 Day 1
Add "ai" or "ay":
ai, ay, ai, ay, ai
ay, ai, ay, ai, ay
Finish each sentence with a word from above:
paint
play, rain
hay, grain
tray

How much does it cost?
45 cents 85 cents
30 cents $1.05
Count backwards by 5s:
95, 85, 75, 65, 55
45, 35, 25, 15, 5

Go to www.SummerFitLearning.com for Additional Games, Trivia, and Activities!

Week 6 Day 2
Don't forget your manners:
hello, nice, sorry, open, thank you, sorry,
excuse me, may

Unscramble the letters:
please, excuse me
thank you, may I

Week 6 Day 2
Measure using centimeters: 12 cm, 3.5 cm,
5 cm, 4.5 cm, 3.5 cm, 6.5 cm

Week 6 Day 3
Circle the needs:
Shoe, house, watermelon, apple, soap
Mittens, clothes, carrot
Cross off the wants:
Hamburger, soda, boat, soda, candy, toys, ball

Write the number that comes before:
49, 13, 20, 7
25, 36, 75, 9
Write the number that comes between:
10, 26, 52
20, 68, 80
Finish the pattern:
3, 9, 15, 21,, 27
Circle the largest number, cross of the
smallest in each row:
66, 36
98, 38

Week 6 Day 4
Classifying:, chicken, ram, corn, skis, cupcake,
toad, top, foot, pig

[draw minutes on clocks]
Write the temperatures:
45 degrees, 80 degrees, 30 degrees
[color 1 crab]
Circle the correct answer(s):
seat
black
courage
herself & everyone on the bus

Week 6 Day 5
seat, black, courage, everyone on the bus

Week 7 Day 1
Abbreviations:
Doctor – Dr.
Mister – Mr.
Misses – Mrs.
Street – St.
Senior – Sr.
January – Jan.
Sunday – Sun.
Wednesday – Wed.
August – Aug.
October – Oct.
Friday – Fri.
February – Feb.
Saturday – Sat.
Tuesday – Tue.
September – Sept.
November – Nov.

Finish the fact family:
9 − 5 = 4, 9 − 4 = 5
7 + 3 = 10
3 + 7 = 10
10 − 7 = 3
10 − 3 = 7
How many frogs are left on the log:
5 frogs are left because 8 − 3 = 5

Week 7 Day 2
People in our communities:
mail carrier, doctor, grocer, teacher, dentist,
police officer, firefighter

Map of Franklin Park:
East
Duck Pond
Franklin Park
North

Week 7 Day 3
Fill in with "ch" or "sh" to complete each
word:
sh, ch, ch, sh
sh, sh, ch, sh
Change the asking sentences to telling
sentences:
We are going to the beach.
The chicken crossed the road.
Change the telling sentences to asking
sentences:
Is the ship sailing across the sea?
Can you climb up the peach tree?

[Color in the graph]
8 + 10 = 18
5 − 3 = 2
6 + 5 = 11

Week 7 Day 4
Name the four oceans:
Pacific Ocean, Atlantic Ocean, Indian Ocean,
Arctic Ocean
North America
Asia
Australia
North America
Asia

Circle the sum or difference:
five
ten
seven
six
1 tens 5 ones, 1 ten 8 ones
2 tens, 1 one, 1 ten, 9 ones
Count backwards by 10s:
90, 80, 70, 50, 40, 30, 10
Fill in the blanks to complete the sentences:
India
war
respect

Week 7 Day 5
India, war, respect

Week 8 Day 1
Color each set of fish with sound-alike words
the same color:
be, bee
too, two, to
meat, meet
son, sun
bare, bear
pear, pair
four, for
nose, knows
sea, see

Odd or even:
odd numbers = green
even numbers = blue

Week 8 Day 2
My family tree:
[fill in tree]

My important numbers:
[fill in numbers]
Finish the pattern:
A,B,A,B,A,B, A,B,A,B,A,B
1, 2, 3, 1, 2, 3, 1, 2, 3, 1, 2, 3

Answers

Week 8 Day 3
Pronouns:
she
they
we
it
he, them
her
them

Draw a line from each alien to the spaceship:
11 – 1, 12 – 2, 15 – 5, 16 – 6, 18 – 8, 19 – 9,
17 – 7, 14 – 4, 13 – 3
Circle the bank with the most money:
[circle first bank = 76 cents]

Week 8 Day 4
Circle the healthy foods:
pretzel, apple, cheese
milk, bread, corn
banana, carrot
 [draw picture of healthy meal]

Circle the best estimate:
95 cents, $10.00, $1.00
$15.00, 80 cents, $15,000.00
What time will it be in 1 hour:
2:00

Week 8 Day 5
Draw yourself being responsible.

Week 9 Day 1
Fill in the names of each symbol:
American flag
Liberty Bell
Statue of Liberty
Mexico
U.S. Capitol
"Star Spangled Banner"
bald eagle
Canada

Draw a line to match the measurements:
1 yard – 3 feet
1 minute – 60 seconds
1 year – 12 months
1 pound – 16 ounces
1 hour – 60 minutes
Complete the equations:
11, 11, 14
How many cents do these coins total:
70 cents
39 cents

Week 9 Day 2
Following directions:
1, 5, 4, 2, 3
4, 5, 3, 2, 1
Write ½ of each number:
5
6
7
8
9
10
Write + or – :
+
-
+
-

Week 9 Day 3
Adjectives:, Blue, Stinky, Slimy, Hot, Soft,
Rainy, Spotted

What time is it?
8:20, 5:10, 6:45
[circle 12 bagels]
Count by 10s:
130, 150, 170, 190

Week 9 Day 4
bone
doll
book
mittens
corn
tomatoes
Write <, >,or =:
>, <
=, <
<, =

[write tally marks]
How many children were swimming at the
pool?
9 + 8 = 17
Fill in the blanks using words from the box:
shark, arm
fear
surf
dreams

Week 9 Day 5
shark, arm, fear, surf, dreams

Week 10 Day 1
Fill in the missing letters "oa" or "ou":
oa, ou, oa
oa, ou, oa
ou, oa, oa
[read sight words]

Match coins with object:
49 cents – apple
65 cents – pretzel
75 cents – candy
95 cents – toy car
Fill in the missing numbers:
4, 8, 12, 16, 20, 24, 28
15, 25, 35, 45, 55, 65, 75

Week 10 Day 2
At the beach:, pail, sunglasses, ball, umbrella,
waves, sand castle, starfish, shovel

Color one equal part:
¼, 1/6, ½
Write the before and after numbers by 5s:
20, 30; 10, 20; 55, 65
Write the differences to solve the equations:
20   40
20   50
10   20
0   40

Week 10 Day 3
Busy as a Beaver:
brown
plants and trees
lodge
paddle
in lakes and streams
dam

Circle the correct answer:
60   24
12   12
Write the numbers from least to greatest
80, 108, 118, 180, 188
Complete the pattern:
16, 18, 20
12, 15, 18

Week 10 Day 4
[write your story]

Draw 2 flowers in each vase:
5 vases; 2 flowers; 10 flowers in all
[color digits]
[match pictures to names]

Week 10 Day 5
draw a line to the accompanying picture

CONGRATULATIONS!

your name

Has completed
Summer Fit 1-2

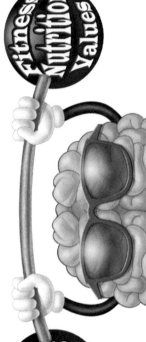

and is ready for the 2nd grade.

Parent or guardian's signature